Mathew Carey, Pennsylvania General Assembly

Debates and Proceedings of the General Assembly of Pennsylvania

on the memorials praying a repeal or suspension of the law annulling the charter of the bank

Mathew Carey, Pennsylvania General Assembly

Debates and Proceedings of the General Assembly of Pennsylvania
on the memorials praying a repeal or suspension of the law annulling the charter of the bank

ISBN/EAN: 9783337123789

Printed in Europe, USA, Canada, Australia, Japan

Cover: Foto ©Suzi / pixelio.de

More available books at **www.hansebooks.com**

DEBATES and PROCEEDINGS

OF THE

GENERAL ASSEMBLY

OF

PENNSYLVANIA,

ON THE MEMORIALS PRAYING A REPEAL OR SUSPENSION OF THE LAW ANNULLING THE CHARTER OF THE BANK.

MATHEW CAREY, EDITOR.

PHILADELPHIA:

PRINTED FOR CAREY AND Co. SEDDON AND PRITCHARD.

M.DCC.LXXXVI.

To his EXCELLENCY BENJAMIN FRANKLIN, PRESIDENT of the COMMONWEALTH of PENNSYLVANIA, L. L. D. &c. &c.

HONOURED SIR,

PERMIT me to dedicate to you these *primitiæ* or first fruits of the eloquence of a commonwealth which your fostering hand has happily conducted from childhood to maturity.

These debates afford a pleasing prospect that Pennsylvania will, in process of time, behold her senate adorned with orators not inferior, perhaps, to those boasts of antiquity—Demosthenes, Isocrates, Cicero, &c. &c.

Your celebrity as a philosopher—a statesman—and (a higher title than either) a citizen of the world, would receive no addition from the most elaborate eulogium I could write. I shall forbear, therefore, to tread the beaten track of dedicators; and shall rest content with uniting my sincere wishes with those of your admiring and grateful countrymen, that every felicity which heaven bestows upon the most favoured of the human race, may await you while you abide in this terrestrial habitation——and that your memory may be revered and cherished by the friends of science ---of liberty---and benevolence, till time shall cease to be.

I am, sir, with due esteem,

Your most obedient humble servant,

MATHEW CAREY.

Philadelphia, April 20, 1786.

IN the following debates, the same arguments frequently occur twice, and, in some few instances, perhaps a third or fourth time. The editor anticipates a question which will, doubtless, be asked by most of the readers, viz. " Why, in " those cases, he has not rested satisfied with the first state-" ment, and omitted the others ?" To this he answers, that when introduced again in the manner above mentioned, they are mostly considered in a different point of view, and some new lights thrown upon them. Moreover, the importance of the subject inspired him with a desire of laying the debates before the public in as ample a manner as possible. Still further : If he had suppressed any part of the members' speeches, he would have subjected himself to the charge of partiality, which he has studiously endeavoured to avoid.

It will be remarked, that the answers to some of the arguments, state them differently from what they appear in the original speeches. This has sometimes arisen from one member mistaking the meaning of another : sometimes, the fault lies with the editor.

As to omissions, he must be chargeable with them in various places. He does not understand short hand, without which it is utterly impossible to keep pace with a speaker, unless he delivers himself very leisurely. However, he flatters himself that very few of the material arguments on either side, have escaped him.

Whatever may be the defects or imperfections of the pamphlet, they will, he trusts, be readily excused, when it is considered that his chief object has been to contribute to the information of the public, on a subject of as great magnitude, perhaps, as any agitated in this state since the revolution.

Philadelphia, April 20, 1786

Debates and Proceedings, &c.

General Assembly of Pennsylvania.

Friday, March 3, 1786, A. M.

A memorial signed by 624 inhabitants of the city and liberties of Philadelphia, was presented to the chair, and read as follows:

To the honourable the representatives of the freemen of the commonwealth of Pennsylvania, in general assembly met,

IMPRESSED with a just sense of the inestimable blessing of freedom, and considering, as we ought, that an impartial administration of justice is the fundamental principle of the constitution, and that the security of property, be it little or much, or to whoever it may belong, is one of the chief ends of government; we conceive it to be our bounden duty to watch over the conduct of those, whom our free suffrages, as a free people, have entrusted with the management of public affairs, so as at all times to guard against a remissness of duty, or a wanton or incautious exercise of power on their part.

Impressed, we say, with these ideas and principles, we are led to state to this honourable house, a matter, in which, as it appears on the printed minutes of the late house of assembly, there has not been that proper and impartial attention paid, which the principles of the constitution and the true end of government require.

The case we refer to is as follows:

On the 21st of March last, petitions from sundry inhabitants of Chester county were presented to the house and read.

read. Those petitions began by stating a number of charges and allegations against the bank of North America, but without making or offering proof or evidence of their being true; and praying that the charter of said bank may be repealed.

On the 23d in the morning, two other petitions to the same purport were presented and read for the first time, and read again for the second time on the same day: whereupon, on motion made and seconded, they were referred to a committee to enquire and report thereon.

We conceive it to be an indispensible principle, whenever the property of any of the citizens of this commonwealth is to be affected by the charges and allegations of any man or number of men, that the charges and allegations shall be proved, and that the party so charged and accused shall be heard in its defence; and that it is a departure from the principles of the constitution, for the representatives of the people to take any such charges and allegations as matters of truth, without proof or evidence of their being so; and that for any house of assembly to proceed thereon, to the injury of the property of any of our fellow-citizens, without evidence had, and defence heard, is unconstitutional, and that no law so obtained or passed can be operative, because it is repugnant to the principles of justice and the constitution.

Your memorialists are deeply concerned to have occasion to observe, (and as citizens are deeply interested in the observation) that it does not appear, either from the report of the committee to whom the said petitions, charges, and allegations were committed, or from any other proceedings of the late house of assembly, that any enquiry was made, or any proof or evidence had or produced of the said charges and allegations being true: yet the said house proceeded to bring in a bill, which has in it the nature of a *sentence*, on the *supposed* truth of the said charges and allegations, instead of enquiring into and ascertaining them by proof and evidence— the title of which bill is, *An act to repeal an act of* " *assembly, entitled,* " An act to incorporate the subscribers " to the bank of North America, &c."

Your memorialists are further concerned to observe, that when the persons whose property was immediately to be affected by the passing this bill into a law, applied by petition to be heard in their defence, and, of consequence, against the said charges and allegations, on the *supposed* truth of which, the aforesaid bill was founded: the said house refused

fused to hear them, thereby denying them that right which every citizen of this commonwealth is entitled to.

Your memorialists find by the printed minutes of the late house, April 4th, that when the said bill was called up for a second reading, a motion was made by mr. Pettit, and seconded by mr. Willing, that the memorial of the president, directors, and company of the bank of North America, praying to be heard, be read; and on the question that the prayer of the said memorial be granted, it was negatived. See April 4th, page 284.

Your memorialists think it right to remark, that those proceedings of the late house, and of their committee, afford a strong presumption to many good citizens, that the charges and allegations against the bank are ill founded, and not true; and that other causes than those which have been assigned, are to be looked for, as the true causes for the vehement attack on the bank.

Your memorialists further find by the said printed minutes (April 4th, p. 284) that immediately after the said prayer, " to be heard," was rejected, the house went into the second reading of the said bill, without any enquiry into the truth of the charges and allegations aforesaid; and having finished the said second reading, the bill, as is usual, was ordered to be published for public consideration.

On this part of the proceedings, your memorialists conceive it their duty, as well as their right as citizens, to remark—

That the publishing the bill for the public to consider upon, without (the house) having first investigated the charges and allegations against the bank, which were the moving causes of the proceedings of the house, and on the *supposed* truth of which the said bill was founded, and without hearing the defence of the parties so charged and alleged against, was bringing the bill before the public in a very partial and incomplete manner; because it was leaving the public in the dark as to the truth or existence of the matters on which their consideration was to be exercised; and withholding from them the knowledge on which their judgment was to be formed. It was impossible the public could, by any consideration of theirs, determine or know, whether the matters charged on the bank were true or false. Consideration has no proper object to go upon, when applied to charges without evidence, and still less so when applied to a sentence, without having both the evidence and the defence.

The bill, then ordered to be published, had in it the nature of a sentence, and nothing can appear to us more inconsistent than the publishing a sentence for the consideration of the public, and for the purpose of obtaining the concurrence or opinion of the public thereon, and suppressing the matters on which that sentence is founded.

Your memorialists are much concerned to find such deviations from, if not direct violations of, the constitution; and that within so short a time after the late convention had pointed out defects of a similar nature in the conduct of former assemblies.

Your memorialists are further induced to observe—that on the question itself, respecting the repealing the charter of the bank, they feel themselves under some uneasy sensations and apprehensions. At any rate, it is breaking the word and promise of the state, publicly pledged but a short time before—a measure, which at first view holds out to the world a faithless disposition in Pennsylvania, and puts all kind of credit, public and private, on a precarious footing—a measure, of which the power to do it may be litigated, because it may be made a question, whether any law can warrant the doing an unlawful thing. Therefore the repealing a charter, being a step of the utmost delicacy and danger, requires to be gone into with the nicest care, and the most cautious and scrupulous investigation. If any causes can justify such proceeding, those causes ought to be made visible to the world, or our credit with the world is wounded, if not ended. For, who will trust a government that assumes the power of breaking its word, or will trust the individuals of a country that live under such a government? The paper money of one house may be voted down by the next; and the engagements of one assembly be superceded by its successors. It will be of little use to us afterwards, to say, that any number or party of the assembly, were the persons who did it. Those persons may be returned to the rank of private citizens, or departed the state, when the mischiefs they shall have occasioned, shall take place.

But your memorialists are distressed to observe, that instead of caution and investigation, instead of precision and deliberation, they find the business taken up on the slightest grounds, and conducted with a spirit of haste and precipitancy extremely ill-suited to the nature and importance of the subject.

Your

Your memorialists find by the printed minutes of the late house, that the petitions against the bank were read twice in the same day, referred to a committee to enquire and report thereon, and the report of that committee delivered in, not the very next day, but the day after,—That report read a first and second time, debated and resolved upon, and a second committee appointed to bring in a bill, and that bill brought in and read, and all this within the space of six days, viz. from the 23d to the 29th of March; for the truth of which we refer to the printed minutes of the house.

When we consider the extensive nature of the case, the variety of knowledge necessary to collect, to form a judgment upon, and the probable danger of such a proceeding to public and private credit, we must declare upon our own knowledge and opinion of the nature of the subject, that neither the time, nor the attention bestowed, was equal to the importance of it.

Your memorialists find, that the late house of assembly having neglected to enquire into the truth of the charges and allegations against the bank, and yet taken up these charges and allegations as true, refusing at the same time to grant the prayer of the proprietors of the bank to be heard in their defence, published the aforesaid bill, for, what is called, public consideration, and adjourned soon after to the 23d of August following.

As the said bill, during the recess of the house, was before the public in the imperfect state we have already mentioned, it was impossible for the public to form any judgment upon it, because the facts and matters on which they were to judge, were withheld from them, and therefore the publication of it could not answer the purposes intended by the constitution: But if any judgment is to be formed from the general elections which took place soon after the passing this bill, we may conclude it met with great disapprobation, because so many of the members who voted for it, have been displaced by their constituents; and we cannot doubt that as this darksome business comes to be better known, and more illuminated, and the true interest of Pennsylvania fuller understood, that a more extensive reprobation will take place; for it is natural that a free people should abhor the reproach of being a faithless one, and impossible they should countenance a measure which has the appearance of despotism.

Your memorialists find, that on the meeting of the late house for their last sitting, on the 23d of August, the president, directors and company of the bank of North-America, renewed their application to the houfe for a hearing; and that a petition from eight perfons, (figners to the petitions for repealing the charter of the bank) viz. James Pearfon, Robert Smith, William Graham, John Barker, John Kling, George Leib, Levi Budd, and Frederick Heimberger, was likewife prefented to the houfe, praying to be heard in fupport of their petitions, both which requefts were complied with.

Your memorialifts find by the minutes of the late houfe, page 356, that on the fifth of September, the day appointed by the houfe for a hearing, the prefident of the bank prefented himfelf perfonally at the bar of the houfe, and likewife by counfel; but it does not appear from the faid minutes, that any of the perfons who had figned the petitions, charges and allegations againft the bank, appeared perfonally to fupport and prove them; neither does it appear that they produced fo much as a fingle evidence to prove what they had figned to, or attempted to prove it.

If therefore they have figned to charges and allegations which are not true, and the houfe have acted on thofe charges and allegations as if they were true, there is a manifeft injury committed; and as reparation is due to the injured, as well as to the injured honor of the ftate, your memorialifts confide that this hon. houfe will take fuch meafures as may make the neceffary reparation.

The charges and allegations on the part of the petitioners againft the bank, not being attempted to be proved, the bank could only deny them; and we find by the minutes of the houfe, that the matter ended in a verbal litigation between a counfel on each fide, inftead of going into an inveftigation and proof of the charges advanced, on the fuppofed truth of which the houfe had acted.

On this part of the bufinefs, your memorialifts think it neceffary to obferve, that the refufing the bank a hearing in the firft ftage of the bufinefs, before the bill was publifhed for public confideration, and admitting the bank to a hearing at the very latter part of the feffion, was precluding the judgment of the public upon the cafe, becaufe the publication of the bill, and the time for public confideration, was paffed; and no new matter which any hearing at that time might produce, could have time or opportunity to be publicly known.

Had the hearing been before the fecond reading of the bill, and confequently before it was to be publifhed for public confideration, which was the requeft the bank made, the

public

public would then have known, that the petitioners against the bank had not proved their charges and allegations; and this would have been matter for the public to have exercised their consideration and judgment upon: but of this they were precluded by their representatives.

That the charges and allegations against the bank are ill-grounded and not true, is naturally to be inferred from their not being proved nor attempted to be proved—And that the prayer of the petitioners against the bank is founded on very ill and dangerous principles, subversive of the good of society, and of the fundamentals of the constitution, and of all true government, is best inferred from the prayer itself, which we here subjoin:

"Therefore," say the petitioners, "in order to restore public confidence and private security, we pray, that a bill may be brought in, and passed into a law, for repealing the law for incorporating the bank."—On which we remark, that nothing can be more dangerous in principle and practice, and more absurd and monstrous, than to pray that the government may break its word, in order to be the better believed and trusted, and violate the confidence already placed in it, in order that the people may place more: yet such is the exact prayer of their petition, for the truth of which we appeal to the printed minutes of the house, and likewise to the petition itself.

These are the subject matters which your memorialists have to lay before your honorable house; they are concerned there should be any occasion to do it, and still more concerned there should be so much. The watching over the conduct of the representatives is the proper duty of the citizens of a free country, and in presenting this memorial we discharge the duty incumbent on us.

We therefore pray your honorable house, that these matters may be taken into your most serious consideration, and that either the repealing law may be repealed, or a bill be brought in, to suspend the operation of it, until your hon. house can obtain full information on the subject.

And your memorialists, &c.

Ordered to lie on the table.

N. B. On different days afterwards, sundry similar memorials were presented to the house.

Wednesday,

Wednesday, March 15, 1786, A. M.

Read a second time, the memorials praying a repeal or suspension of the law, annulling the Charter of the bank.

Ordered, that they, together with the petitions against the bank, presented to the late house of Assembly, be referred to Messrs. Clymer, Robinson, Lilly, Rittenhouse, and Edgar, to report thereon.

Thursday, March 23, 1786, A. M.

Mr. Clymer, as Chairman of the above Committee, presented to the speaker the following report:

The Committee to whom were referred the memorials of the citizens of Philadelphia and other parts, setting forth the irregular and partial conduct of the late house of Assembly, in repealing the Charter of the bank of North-America, and praying for a restoration thereof, or a suspension of the repealing act,—report,

THAT the said memorials containing a statement of proceedings, adduced by the memorialists in support of their charges against the late house—your committee first had recourse to the printed minutes, and found the statement had been truly made.

That conceiving it more their duty to state facts than opinions, your committee, in order to obtain information as to the reality of the complaints alleged against the bank in certain petitions presented to the late house, applied to Mr. Whitehill and Mr. Smilie, members of a committee appointed by that house to *enquire* therein, and on whose report a bill was brought in to repeal the said charter; and requested to know what were the enquiries they had made in consequence: but those gentlemen in answer to a question put to them, said, they had not called at the bank to make themselves acquainted with the nature of the transactions there: and your committee inferred generally from their conversation, that neither they, the said Mr. Whitehill and Mr. Smilie, nor any of their colleagues, had made any special or occasional enquiry whatever concerning the bank.

The memorials mentioning the names of eight persons who had stood forth as supporters of the petitions against the bank, four of them, viz. Messieurs James Pearson, Robert Smith, William Graham, and Frederick Heimberger, attending your committee in pursuance of notifications sent to them,

them, they the said four persons were questioned as to facts relating to the bank consistent with their own knowledge: but they declined satisfying your committee further than that they had not been at the bank to gain information.

The president and some of the directors of the bank also attending at the request of your committee, they affirmed that none of the members of the committee of the late house, or any of all the petitioners, had ever asked information at the bank concerning the conduct of that institution, or the nature of its transactions, though they the said president and directors had at all times been ready to give such information, and had invited free enquiry.

It will follow from this relation, that the report made to the late house, was grounded in general notions preconceived, or on the current popular opinions and speculations, without much consideration being bestowed on the special subject; and the same may at least be said of the petitions presented against the bank.

It will follow also that the house did not derive from either members of that committee, or the said petitioners, those clear lights which would have been necessary to their deliberations on so difficult and interesting a subject, and which from the instructions to their committee, they seem to have desired.

Your committee on examining further into the conduct of the late house, in this transaction, could not but discover, in some instances, a spirit little suited to the transient and accountable representatives of a free people. In an early stage of the business, and when only it could have had its use, the bank was denied a hearing: and when at a later stage, it was yielded to the repeated instances of its president and directors, the permission was qualified with this remark, "that it must be considered as a matter of *favour* " and not of right." But the favour became nugatory through the application of a rule of order, which, obliging the council for the bank to speak before the council for the petitioners, left him to combat in the dark against possible charges and conjectural imputations. True it is, he was suffered to make a reply to the adverse counsel, but within a time so limited by the house, as could scarcely be sufficient for preparation in any petty cause in the ordinary courts.

Thus confining themselves to facts and to reflections naturally arising from them, your committee conceive the conduct of the late house, in the instance of the bank, to be of
most

moſt dangerous example. In their precipitancy, they broke through the procraſtinating forms of proceeding, which were fixed as fences againſt the ſudden violences of power. And in their partiality they appear to have manifeſted a pre-determination to condemn.

Your committee beg leave to remark on ſome circumſtances attending the memorials preſented to this houſe, which ought to have confiderable weight in their preſent deliberations. The ſubſcribers to theſe memorials are ſo numerous as to beſpeak the general ſenſe of the community. In them are included the moſt reſpectable characters amongſt us; men who, from their intercourſe and condition in life, muſt be ſuppoſed beſt experienced in the effects, good or bad, produced by the operations of the bank, and from general knowledge moſt intelligent in the nature of ſuch inſtitutions.

As the proceedings of the late houſe in the caſe of the bank, thus appear with all the marks of precipitancy, prejudice and partiality, the annulling act has its foundation deeply laid in injuſtice, and remains a reproach both to the government and to the people. But your committee truſting in the wiſdom and probity of the preſent houſe, to reſtore to the ſtate its loſt honour, ſubmit the following reſolution :

That a ſpecial committee be appointed to prepare and bring in a bill to repeal an act, entitled, " An act to repeal
" an act of aſſembly, entitled, An act to incorporate the ſub-
" ſcribers to the bank of North America, alſo one other
" act, entitled, An act for preventing and puniſhing the
" counterfeiting of the common ſeal, bank bills and bank
" notes of the preſident, directors, and company of the
" bank of North America, and for other purpoſes therein
" mentioned."

GEO. CLYMER.
Wᴍ. ROBINSON, junr.
JOSEPH LILLY.

Read, and ordered to lie on the table.

Ordered that Wedneſday next be aſſigned for the ſecond reading of the above report.

Wedneſday,

Wednesday, March 29, 1786, A. M.

AGREEABLY to the order of the day, took up for a second reading, the report of the committee to whom were referred the memorials praying a repeal or suspension of the law for annulling the charter of the bank.

Mr. R. Morris having enquired the number of signers to the petitions presented to the late house of assembly relative to the bank, and to the memorials in favour of the bank, presented to the present house, they appeared as follow:

Petitions against the bank presented to the late house, signed by 1199 persons.

Petitions in favour of the bank, presented to the late house signed by 608 persons, of whom 516 were of the city of Philadelphia.

Memorials in favour of the bank presented to the present house, signed by 2947 persons.

The report being read,

Mr. Robinson addressed himself to the speaker as follows: In discussing the present question, two principal considerations arise: first, by what authority a legislature can dissolve a charter solemnly granted to any institution: and secondly, the utility or the bad consequences of the particular institution. I shall not go into both. As a member of the committee who have made the report before the house, I shall explain the ground of their proceeding, and shall consider but one of those points; the power to dissolve a charter. The committee formed their conclusions from a conviction that the legislature has not that power. To decide this, two questions arise. In what capacity the legislature acts in granting charters of incorporation? And in what capacity in taking them away? In granting charters the legislature acts in a ministerial capacity. In this proposition I am supported by the constitution. The ninth section of the frame of government states—that the assembly " shall sit on their
" own adjournments; prepare bills and enact them into laws;
" judge of the elections and qualifications of their own mem-
" bers: they may expel a member, but not a second time
" for the same cause; they may administer oaths or affirma-
" tions on the examinations of witnesses; redress grievances;
" impeach state criminals; grant charters of incorporation;
" constitute towns, boroughs, and counties." All these, dif-
fering

fering in themselves, are acts of the legislature. Some are for preparing general regulations, which extend to all the state; these are laws. They judge of the qualifications of their own members. Their sentence is not a law.—Their granting charters is an act of agency—in which they have a power to act for the community, whose agents they are appointed. This is totally distinct from the power of making laws, and it is a novel doctrine in Pennsylvania that they can abrogate those charters so solemnly granted. There is this grand distinction between laws and charters of incorporation granted by the legislature.—The first are general rules, which extend to the whole community—the second bestow particular privileges upon a certain number of people. It is unnecessary to dwell long upon this matter, as I propose merely to trace the ground of the proceedings of the committee. The second question which offers itself to us, is, in what capacity the legislature acts in taking away a charter? In this they act judicially. They hear the cause, and determine on its merits. Now this exceeds their powers. They are not authorised by the constitution to act in a judicial capacity, but so far as regards the qualifications of their own members—and in some few other matters, so as to preserve themselves from insult—such as in case of disturbances in the house; for they could not secure themselves from insult, if they could not take cognizance of the matter immediately. These are their only judicial powers. They are not competent to decisions in cases of property. Charters are a species of property. When they are obtained, they are of value. Their forfeiture belongs solely to the courts of justice. The constitution says, " that in controversies respecting property, the " party shall have a trial by jury." But the late house stepped between the president and directors of the bank, and their rights, and deprived them of the legal mode of trial. In this an essential injury has been done them. The house presumed upon its own power, and that it must be obeyed —and upon the weakness of the other party. Let no man say, that tyranny cannot exist in a large assembly. It may become a many-headed hydra, as fond of power as individuals. It is not the nature of mankind to give up what power they possess. They are fond of keeping, and even sometimes of exceeding it. With even the best intentions, a legislature may go beyond the proper bounds, and be deceived into an opinion of possessing powers they never were vested with. In a free government like ours, it is particularly

larly incumbent on us to prevent the attempts of an exorbitant power. The conſtitution has ſet bounds to the power of the legiſlature, and ſaid, " thus far ſhalt thou go, and no " farther." Unleſs they break the original and fundamental principles of the conſtitution, they cannot pretend to a power of taking away charters. Perhaps it will be ſaid, with Blackſtone, that charters of incorporation may be forfeited by an act of parliament or of aſſembly. He holds the power of an act of parliament to be unbounded. But though this might be his opinion, it does not follow that it is juſt: far otherwiſe. The more eaſy it is to make it obeyed, the more caution is neceſſary to avoid injuſtice. Moſt common law writers before Blackſtone appear of a different opinion, by their ſilence reſpecting this method. And even he appears to imply, it was power not right that did it. The only modes, therefore, by which charters can be vacated, are: 1ſt. by death of the members of the corporation—2dly, by reſignation of right—and 3dly, by forfeiture in the courts of juſtice. As to the firſt, nothing is neceſſary to be ſaid. The ſecond is voluntary, and a ſpecies of legal ſuicide. And the third is the only legal mode in which charters can be taken away in this country. The principles of our conſtitution are materially different from thoſe of the Britiſh conſtitution.—Here they are clearly defined. In Great Britain, an act of parliament has all the force of the conſtitution. In this country, the different ſpecies of power are diſtributed to different bodies. If the original principles be broken, by one branch of government paſſing beyond the bounds which ſeparate it from the other, liberty cannot long exiſt.

What is the manner of enquiry on trials, in the courts of juſtice? The evidences are brought, and the parties are preſent to examine them. Has this been the caſe with the bank? Had the parties intereſted in that inſtitution, an opportunity to examine the evidence againſt them? No. Charges were brought, but no evidence to ſupport them. The charges might be true, or might not. But as the neceſſary forms were not obſerved, it follows that there was a ſentence given without any proof being made. The ninth ſection of the bill of rights declares, that a man charged with any crime, ſhall be heard by himſelf and counſel. Yet when the preſident and directors of the bank requeſted to be heard by counſel, in an early ſtage of the bill, they were refuſed: and when at length it was granted, it was declared a

matter

matter of favour—not of right. True, if the house, when it acts in a legiflative capacity, hears counfel, it may be faid to be a matter of favour. But when it affumed the power of acting in a judicial capacity, it was a matter of indifpenble right that the parties fhould be heard. The act of affembly relative to the bank, carries with it all the confequences of an act of attainder—and awards a fentence, without hearing whether the charter was forfeited or not. From all thefe confiderations, it fully appears that the houfe of affembly had not fuch judicial powers as would be competent to decide on the cafe of the bank : and even if they had, their proceedings were not conducted with the regularity or order requifite. Thefe were the inducements on which the committee framed their report—and thefe inducements will, I hope, be fufficient to make the houfe agree to it.

Mr. Lollar faid, when the gentleman rofe, he expected he meant, as one of the committee, to explain to the houfe their reafons for making fuch a report. But he had not done it to his fatisfaction, and therefore he fhould make a few obfervations : one in particular on the report. Had the committee confined themfelves to the memorials, without cafting any reflections on the late affembly, they would have acted much better than they had done. But their report as it ftood, was a declaration of war againft the late houfe, and daring to the combat all fuch of its members as were in the prefent. If he had gone about to caft reflections, it fhould have been on the affembly that granted the charter, not on the affembly that took it away. It was not founded in juftice. But the houfe which granted it, entertained no idea of its being for a perpetuity, or of its being out of the power of the affembly to alter or new model it, as they might fee fit. In fupport of this, mr. Lollar quoted the minutes of that houfe, where it appeared that a claufe had been introduced as a rider to the bill, for the purpofe of empowering the affembly that fhould fit in 1789, to alter or amend the charter, as might be neceffary. This was rejected by 27 to 24, and the exprefs reafon affigned for the rejection, was, that the charter of the bank muft neceffarily be always within the power of the houfe. Mr. Lollar then faid, that a law whereby the corporation had an unlimited fucceffion, was unjuft—and the annulling it highly proper. Thus matters were brought on the broad bottom of equality. The Charter was moreover unjuft, as the ftate had got no equivalent for the advantages it had beftowed : and civilians held that in all

contracts,

contracts, unlefs there was an equivalent received for what was given, the bargain or agreement was void in itfelf, and incomplete. The only confideration received from the bank, was, that it facilitated commerce. This in the prefent fituation of the affairs of the ftate, was againft it: as it was an engine of trade that enabled the merchants to import more goods than were neceffary, or than there was money to pay for. This was clearly difadvantageous. The learned counfel who had pleaded the caufe of the bank, before the late affembly, had candidly and ingenuoufly admitted, that when the balance of trade was againft a country, a bank was injurious. Mr. Lollar then quoted the petitions prefented to the late houfe againft the bank, in thefe words: " the directors of the bank are enabled to give fuch prefer-
" ences in trade, by advances of money to their particular
" favourites, when moft needed, as to deftroy that equality
" which ought to take place in a commercial country." He faid thefe words were fo plain, it was not neceffary to fay any more on that part of the ill confequences refulting from the bank. He did not mean to fpeak difrefpectfully of the prefent directors—any others in their fituation, he believed, would do as they did. He begged the attention of the houfe to another matter: under the old government, when there were people in the management of affairs as wife or perhaps wifer than thofe fince, no idea had been ever entertained of a bank. Now if it would be a means of keeping the cafh in the country, as had been ftated, it was ftrange it had efcaped their obfervation. But the beft way of promoting the good of this country, that had ever yet been found out, was by paper money, emitted through the medium of a loan office. Of this governor Pownal had fpoken in the following terms: " I will venture to fay, that there never was a wifer
" or a better meafure, never one better calculated to ferve
" the ufes of an increafing country; that there never was a
" meafure more fteadily purfued, or more faithfully execut-
" ed, for forty years together, than the Loan-office in Penn-
" fylvania, formed and adminiftered by the affembly of that
" province." After all expedients fhould be tried, that would be found the only effectual one. He faid, that by means of a bank the European merchants were enabled to procure and carry off money for their goods: and to fix the payment thereof upon the purchafers in that hafty manner which the rules of the bank required, the baneful effects of which had been feen and felt in and about the city.—Whereas if it were

not

not in exiftence, they would be obliged to take produce in exchange for them. He hoped the report would be rejected. As a free citizen, he felt himfelf interefted in the matter. He fhould, in his opinion, betray the truft repofed in him, and act againft the dictates of his confcience, if he voted for it.

Mr. Clymer faid, if the gentleman had confidered the matter properly, he would not have thought an explanation requifite of the reafons of the committee, further than was given in the report. He would find that there was a clofe connection between the beginning and end of it. In the firft part, it was ftated, that the memorials had fet forth the mode of proceeding adopted by the late houfe; it was further ftated, that the committee having made the neceffary enquiries, had found that the mode of proceeding fo fet forth, was confirmed by the minutes of the late houfe. There was, therefore, no neceffity for the committee to go into a recapitulation of what was fo fully ftated in the memorials, which were the ground of their proceedings. The report was fufficiently long already.

Mr. Fitzfimons. I was not a member of the committee who made the report now before the houfe, and efteem myfelf no further bound to advocate it, than as it coincides with my own fentiments. I am of opinion, that the committee not only made a proper report, but paid a proper refpect to the truft repofed in them by this houfe. They made enquiries into the ftatement given in the memorials—and the deductions naturally arifing from the refult of thofe enquiries, they laid before the houfe. As this queftion is of the utmoft importance, not only to the interefts of the citizens of Pennfylvania, but to the union in general, I could have wifhed it confined to a narrow ground, that it might be perfectly underftood.—The memorials complain that the former houfe did not proceed with the deliberation neceffary, not only in a cafe of fuch confequence as the prefent muft be acknowledged, but in any cafe whatever. Whether the bank is beneficial or injurious, is not the queftion: but whether the former houfe had fufficient evidence to warrant their proceedings. What may be the opinion of other gentlemen, I do not know. Mine is, that they had not. This is the ground which I think we ought to confine our debates to. But it has already been deviated from. To prove that the former houfe had not the neceffary evidence, we have only to recur to their minutes. By thofe, it appears that the attack on the bank originated by a petition from Chefter county.

county. This petition stated what the petitioners thought injurious in the institution of the bank. Afterwards, other petitions of the same tendency were presented. The house, as in duty bound, referred those petitions to a committee, with directions to enquire into the allegations they contained, in the following words:

" Resolved, That the said petitions be referred to a com-
" mittee, and that the committee be instructed to enquire
" whether the bank established at Philadelphia, be compati-
" ble with the public safety, and that equality which ought
" ever to prevail between the individuals of a republic, and
" to report thereon."

So far the house did their duty. What was the further progress of this business? The committee so appointed made report. But did they in that report state that they had made the enquiry they were directed to make? Did they submit the circumstances that occurred in their enquiry, to the house? No, they did not. They therefore made themselves responsible for the consequences: and I wish their responsibility could be separated from that of the house. Their report contained no information for the house to deliberate upon: it contained merely opinions—and, if we may judge from circumstances, even those opinions were taken up on trust; for the report is drawn up in the hand-writing of a person not of that committee: and, so far as we can decide from similarity of hand-writing, by the same person who framed the petition from Chester county. This is the ground of the proceeding of the present house. If, therefore, it appears that the former house have tried and condemned the president and directors of the bank unheard, it is incumbent on the present house to abrogate their proceedings, and do justice to the injured. And that they did so, is now in proof before us.

As to the justice of the act, if it be introduced in the course of the debate, I shall endeavour to give my opinion on it. It is a serious thing for a legislature to deprive a body of people of their rights in any instance; but very serious, indeed, to deprive them unheard and untried. For the circumstances of this procedure we need only recur to the memorials—From them it will appear that the former house conducted itself with an informality, not only inconsistent with the principles of this government, but with the principles of any government that pretends to freedom.

This is not the first charter which has been taken away in this state. The charter of the college was taken away at

C   a former

a former period. But in that cafe, it was pretended that the charter had been forfeited. Even this was not thought neceffary with refpect to the bank. If fuch be the progrefs of injuftice, there is no telling where it will end. A gentleman has faid the ftatement of the committee is a declaration of war againft members of the late houfe who have feats in the prefent. But if fpeaking the truth be a declaration of war, I hope we fhall ever have men in this houfe poffeffed of fpirit fufficient to declare war in cafe of neceffity. Had the committee been guilty of mif-ftating the facts, or drawing wrong inferences from them, that would have been fufficient ground to criminate them: but this is not afferted.

It is not neceffary to go into an enquiry whether or no the charter was granted improperly. That is not pretended in the repealing act. If the former houfe had thought that good ground, they would have taken it; as they did not, their advocates now cannot avail themfelves of it.

It has been faid that the charter is an eftate entailed: this is not the fact. The property is conftantly transferring: and I believe there has been no day fince the eftablifhment of the bank, but the gentlemen who have hazarded this affertion, might have purchafed fhares in the ftock.

A gentleman who has fpoken againft the report, has told us, that the counfel who pleaded in favour of the bank before the late houfe, conceded that a bank was unfavourable to a nation when the balance of trade was againft her. If the counfel made that conceffion, I will venture to affert, he was not warranted in fo doing by his clients: and it will only ferve to prove, that a gentleman may be not only eminent in his profeffion, but have great general knowledge, without being able to decide on all queftions: for I, who have no pretenfions to that gentleman's knowledge or ability, not only deny the fact, but undertake to prove that it is not well founded. The report of the committee of the late houfe carries a contradiction to this conceffion on the very face of it. It fays the bank has a tendency to accumulate the wealth of the country in the hands of the ftock-holders. I do not mean in this ftage of the bufinefs to detain the houfe, by going into all the arguments that have been offered for and againft the bank. As I fet out upon a narrow ground, I fhall fo conclude.

My view in rifing was to endeavour to confine the arguments to the report of the committee: but as I prefume it will not be adhered to, I referve to myfelf the right of anfwering swering what may be offered in debate by the gentleman opposed to the resolution.

Mr. Smilie. I find myself on this occasion called upon, not only to defend my country, but to account for my own conduct. And here I beg it may be considered, that the gentlemen on the other side of this question, feel interested in it personally. Those gentlemen are to plead for themselves, and to defend their own cause: whereas we on this side have no private interest to serve on the occasion. In judging of our conduct, I hope respect will be had to that consideration.

I shall first make some remarks on the report of the committee, which is now the subject of our discussion. It is in this report stated, that I told the committee, (when asked a question relative to the information procured by the committee of the late house) that " I had not been at the bank " to procure information." This I totally deny. I call upon the gentlemen of the committee for proofs of their assertion.

Mr. Clymer. I rise to affirm the truth of the assertion. Mr. Whitehill, when called upon, answered with much candour. Mr. Smilie was at first very coy and restiff. He declared he esteemed himself not bound to answer any of our questions, and should be prepared to give satisfaction to the house. But having asked him was he at the bank for information? he, upon my honour, answered, " No." Mr. Fitzsimons was present. I call upon that gentleman to declare what he heard.

Mr. Fitzsimons. I am sorry the time of the house should be taken up on so important an occasion, by so trifling a business. But since I find myself called upon, I must inform the house, that I was in the committee room on the day the president and directors of the bank were requested to attend by the committee. And mr. Smilie being also there, was asked several questions. He said he could easily answer, but he did not esteem himself bound : he should be prepared to answer at a proper time. However, being at length asked, had he been at the bank for information, he declared, No.

Here mr. Smilie called upon messrs. Rittenhouse and Edgar, two members of the committee, who had been present at the time alluded to, to declare what had passed. They both said, that he [mr. Smilie] would not answer any questions.

C 2

Mr. Clymer called upon mr. Lilly, another member of the committee, whose declaration was similar to that of mr. Fitzsimons.

Mr. Smilie. This matter cannot be accounted for but on the ground of different parties. Mr. Rittenhouse and mr. Edgar refused to sign the report.

Mr. Clymer. It was read to those gentlemen: and it was their duty, as members of the committee, to point out wherein it was erroneous: but this they did not attempt to do.

Mr. Smilie. Setting aside this point, I shall now proceed to the consideration of the report. One paragraph of it is in these words:

"Your committee, in examining further into the con-
"duct of the late house in this transaction, could not but
"discover, in some instances, a spirit little suited to the
"transient and accountable representatives of a free people.
"In an early stage of the business, and when only it could
"have had its use, the bank was denied a hearing: and
"when, at a later stage, it was yielded to the repeated
"instances of its president and directors, the permission was
"qualified with this remark, *That it must be considered as a*
"*matter of favour, and not of right.* But the favour became
"nugatory, through the application of a rule of order,
"which, obliging the counsel for the bank to speak before
"the counsel for the petitioners, left him to combat in the
"dark, against possible charges and conjectural imputations.
"True it is, he was suffered to make a reply to the adverse
"counsel, but within a time so limited by the house, as
"could scarcely be sufficient for preparation in any petty
"cause in the ordinary courts."

This is one of the most groundless complaints I ever heard, viz. that the president and directors were not heard in the first instance. It was certainly in the discretion of the house whether to hear them on the report of the committee, or on the bill. And I believe it is the practice in England, never to hear petitions till after the second reading of bills; as, until then, it is not known what they may prove to be. This bill, of which we hear so much complaint made, was read the second time in the winter sessions, and then lay over till the fall, a period of nearly five months—was not that a sufficient time for the public to consider on it? Was not counsel then heard against it? Why then is it asserted that it had not a fair discussion? Some remarks have been made on the hearing having been granted not as a matter of right: but it will not be said that the constitution gives any such right to be heard before the house of assembly.

The report goes on to say: " Your committee beg leave
" to remark on some circumstances attending the memorials
" presented to this house, which ought to have considera-
" ble weight in their present deliberations. The subscribers
" to these memorials are so numerous as to bespeak the ge-
" neral sense of the community. In them are included the
" most respectable characters amongst us; men, who, from
" their intercourses and condition in life, must be supposed
" best experienced in the effects, good or bad, produced by
" the operations of the bank, and from general knowledge,
" most intelligent in the nature of such institutions."

What is this great number of subscribers? Two thousand nine hundred and forty-seven. Can this number be said to speak the general sense of the community? The institution of the bank is advantageous to many of the subscribers—and their power and influence, and I believe the influence and terrors of the bank, have been exerted to procure subscribers to those memorials. They were fabricated in this city, prepared, printed, and sent down to the country. It is well known how easy a matter it is to procure signers in the country. We had, a few days since, petitions from Lancaster, Bucks, and Cumberland counties, against the extension of the market-house, procured by the influence of the persons interested against the measure in this city: this sufficiently accounts for the number of memorialists. But admitting that no such means were used, it cannot be said that they speak the general sense of the community. It is an assertion not founded in fact. The committee, indeed, saw the numbers were not sufficient, and they tried to make up the deficiency another way. They inform us, that " in
" them are included the most respectable characters amongst
" us." This is holding out an aristocratical idea. " An
" honest man's the noblest work of God." A democratical government like ours, admits of no superiority. A virtuous man, be his situation what it may, is respectable. If we enquire what constitutes the respectability meant in the report, we shall very probably find it riches. They have more money than their neighbours, and are therefore more respectable.

The report continues: " As the proceedings of the late
" house, in the case of the bank, thus appear with all the
" marks of precipitancy, prejudice and partiality, the an-
" nulling

"nulling act has its foundation deeply laid in injuſtice, "and remains a reproach both to the government and to the "people."

Let us examine whether this act has its foundation laid in injuſtice. For this purpoſe, it is neceſſary to conſider a little the ſubject of charters. I would obſerve, by the bye, that my worthy friend over the way, (Mr. Robinſon) has been puzzling himſelf with Blackſtone, which muſt ever be the caſe with any perſon who takes the negative ſide of the queſtion. And here I will make this conceſſion, that there are charters ſo ſacred, that they cannot be revoked. But there is a material diſtinction between charters—and the opinions of many have been very wrong on that head. When once an error is taken up, men go on a long time in deluſion. There are many things which we now conſider as abſurd, which were formerly venerated, for want of being properly conſidered.—The doctrine of hereditary right, which is now held odious, was once deemed ſacred. There is a ſtrong reaſon, why perſons from Europe are ſo highly prejudiced in favour of charters. In the 12th and 13th centuries, Europe was in the loweſt ſtate of vaſſalage—the people were in ſome meaſure rooted to the ſoil, and ſold with it. While affairs were in that ſituation, the kings and powerful barons granted charters of incorporation, to towns and cities, thereby exempting them from the common vaſſalage of the ſtate, and beſtowing on them particular immunities; thus giving them political exiſtence. Theſe charters were ſacred, becauſe they ſecured to the perſons on whom they were beſtowed, their natural rights and privileges. But there are, ſir, charters of a very different nature. And here it is neceſſary to fix the point of diſtinction. Charters are rendered ſacred, not becauſe they are given by the aſſembly, or by the parliament---but by the objects for which they are given. If a charter is given in a favour of a monopoly, whereby the natural and legal rights of mankind are invaded, to benefit certain individuals, it would be a dangerous doctrine to hold that it could not be annulled. All the natural rights of the people, as far as is conſiſtent with the welfare of mankind, are ſecured by the conſtitution. All charters granting excluſive rights, are a monopoly on the great charter of mankind. The happineſs of the people is the firſt law.

It has been ſaid, that the charges againſt the bank have not been properly proved. But thoſe who recur to the report of the committee of the late houſe, will ſee that proofs were not wanting. A very ſlight reading of the report may

convince

convince gentlemen that the committee were not appointed to see whether the prefident and directors had done their duty. The matter was taken up on a higher ground. The committee were directed to enquire whether or no the bank was compatible with the safety and welfare of the state. This, the houfe, as guardians of the rights and liberties of the people, had a right to examine into. Let us fuppofe for a moment the committee had not made the enquiry---was not the houfe at liberty to confider their report, and as they agreed in opinion with it, to pafs the act recommended in that report? If the houfe had not that right, dreadful would be our fituation indeed. Let us fuppofe a houfe of affembly fo loft to all fenfe of their duty, and fo corrupt, as to give a charter of monopoly to five men, of all our Eaft India trade--to five others, of our trade to Europe---and to five more, of our trade to the Weft Indies---I grant that it is not likely that this will ever happen---but that is nothing to the point. ---If one houfe, I fay, is guilty of this mifchief, and that the next that meets, beholding this monfter in the face of the conftitution, has not power to give redrefs, to what purpofe are annual elections? Corrupt chartered boroughs in Great Britain have eaten up the fpirit of the conftitution. If the houfe cannot afford a remedy, the people muft have recourfe to the means God and nature have given them for redrefs. No good man can wifh this to happen. I hope it never will. The right of the houfe to repeal charters was debated in the council of cenfors---and a member of that body, now in this houfe, and in favour of the bank, conceded the point of right in the legiflature to revoke them.

I fhall mention a cafe, which will fhew that we are not the only people afraid of banks. In Ireland, in the year 1721, a bank was about to be eftablifhed. It was held to be a furprifing fine thing—But after the houfe of commons had maturely confidered of the matter, they came to the following refolution: "Refolved, that if any member of this houfe,
" or commoner of Ireland, fhall prefume to folicit, or en-
" deavour to procure any grant, or to get the great feal put
" to any charter, for erecting a bank in this kingdom, con-
" trary to the declared fenfe and refolution of this houfe, he
" fhall incur their higheft difpleafure, and be deemed to act
" in contempt of the authority of this houfe, and an enemy
" to his country."

[Here Mr. Smilie read an extract from the journals of the Irifh houfe of commons, containing their proceedings on the above bufinefs, from its firft introduction to its final rejection. He then proceeded as follows:]

If a bank was regarded so dangerous in a country, where there was a counterbalance to its influence, how much more so must it be here, where there is no such counterbalance?

The charter of the bank was not taken away for what the president and directors had done—they, I believe, acted as innocently as any others would have done in the same situation.---But it was taken away from a conviction of its dangerous tendency. We lately had a proposal to mortgage the revenues of the state to the bank---thus to get the state into its tramels.

A word or two with respect to paper money. The paper money of the state cannot exist with the bank. And the question is not---whether or no we shall have paper money--- but who shall emit it---the bank or the state? If the bank emits it, it must have the profits. State paper money has been found of the utmost utility, in former times and lately. Had it not been for the last emission of it, the state could not have paid the public creditors. There were no other means; and a number of valuable citizens must have been unpaid their just demands. Considering the difficulties of government, no hesitation can remain in any man's mind, respecting the propriety of emitting paper. If the state is obliged to borrow, she must necessarily pay 6 per cent.---whereas, if she emits on loan, she gains 6 per cent. in her favour. All these advantages we must give up, if we restore that institution.

It is hardly necessary to mention the endeavours used to prevent the emission of paper money by the committee of merchants. These gentlemen must not take it amiss if we style them bankers---as I believe all of them are such. This was at a time of the greatest distress, when the cries of the public creditors were heard by every ear.

It has been said in the course of this debate, that the learned counsel in favour of the bank, conceded, that when the balance of trade is against a nation, a bank is injurious to it. A gentleman from the city has undertaken to deny that this is the case. But I believe that he will find it difficult to disprove it. His assertion controverts the general sense of mankind.

The operations of the bank are prejudicial in a point of view in which I have not yet considered them. They are a discouragement to agriculture, and to improvements in the city. From the establishment of the bank, interest rose from six per cent. to the enormous degree at which we see it at present.

prefent. Ufury has been coeval with the bank. It was not known here before.

A man finds it much more to his advantage to lodge his cash in the bank, than to purchafe with it lots, lands, or houfes. The perfon who has thofe, finds it impoffible to procure money at legal intereft to improve them, and is therefore inclined to fell them—the fame reafon that inclines him to fell, deters others from purchafing—thus the value of lands, houfes, &c. is depreciated.

The former houfe, confidering all thefe things—confidering that the bank ftood in the way of paper money—confidering that a loan-office and it could not exift together—confidering that it was a bar to the improvement of the country, and to agriculture, thought themfelves fully juftified in taking away the charter. And it is equally our duty to leave matters in their prefent fituation. The bank has not fuffered. The ftock-holders have gained enough—In one year they cleared fixteen and a half per cent. Why fhould we injure our country in favour of an inftitution, incompatible with the public welfare? I therefore hope the houfe will agree to let the bank reft where it is, and fupport the paper money of the ftate, from which fo many advantages are derived.

On motion, ordered that the further confideration of the report be poftponed.

Adjourned.

Thurfday, March 30, 1786, A. M.

RESUMED the confideration of the report of the committee to whom were referred the memorials praying a repeal or fufpenfion of the law annulling the charter of the bank.

Mr. Clymer. As I had the honour, mr. Speaker, to be a member of the committee who made the report now under the confideration of the houfe, I think myfelf bound to defend it from fome important charges made againft it. A gentleman [mr. Smilie] has given us to underftand, that the committee proceeded a wrong way, when they ftated that the committee of the late houfe fhould have made enquiries, which they did not. He feems to fay, that the affembly, in the plenitude of their power, might pafs the repealing act without any enquiries——but this is directly in oppofition to the principles laid down by the late affembly themfelves.

themfelves. They exprefsly directed the committee to make enquiry, whether the bank was compatible with the welfare of the ftate. Have this inqueft and prefentment been held? No. The act, therefore, in the very preamble of it, carries a falfehood. What then becomes of the apologift of the proceedings of the late houfe? He afcribes to them greater powers than they pretend to. They faid an enquiry was neceffary. He fays not. The committee having traced out that no enquiry had been made, and having found the proceedings of the late houfe, as well as of their committee, exceptionable, had a right, as freemen, to pafs their judgment on them. I hope we fhall always have men of fufficient fpirit, to fpeak their fentiments freely of the higheft authority in the ftate. For my own part, I have ever fet my face againft a tyrannical abufe of power; and in a proteft in 1779, againft the proceedings in the college bufinefs, I fpoke my fentiments of the then houfe, of which I was a member, as freely as I have done in the report before you, of the late houfe.

I fhall examine fome of the principles whereon is founded the report of laft year. Among the reft, is this, that the balance of trade is againft us, and that therefore the bank muft be injurious. This balance is the metaphyfics of commerce, which few underftand, and which ferve no other purpofe than to difturb the imagination.. In England, Gee and Child wrote much on that fubject. They pretended to demonftrate that the nation would be ruined by certain branches of trade. But as the nation grew richer and richer by them, nothing but experience could prove the fallacy of their arguments. It is a point, which from being fo little underftood, I cannot fuppofe made any impreffion on the committee themfelves; though it had its ufe in the enumeration, as it fwelled the evils attendant on the inftitution.

There are two other principles of more folidity laid down in the report: one is, that the bank may have a pernicious influence—Banks are the neceffary appendages of a certain degree of commerce. Let us fee what are the interefts of commerce, and we fhall then know how its influence, where it has any, will be pointed. It has, then, an evident intereft in the general profperity—in the fecurity of property—and in the toleration of every man to purfue his own benefit in his own way, provided it be not incompatible with the public good. Thefe are the objects which commerce and its banks would endeavour to accomplifh, and they are certainly

tainly not pernicious. The early immunities and privileges bestowed on traders in modern Europe, after the extinction of the Roman empire, were the first seeds of any national liberty which followed. But a gentleman has produced the example of an entire nation opposed to the influence of banks—he has, however, greatly blundered at the application of this example. The Irish nation, in 1721, and many years after, was greatly dependent on England, both in its liberties and trade. In this situation, the establishment of a bank must have been attempted either by the English ministry, further to distress the trade of the country—and therefore opposed by the Irish patriots;—or attempted by those patriots, to relieve their trade from English oppression, and therefore opposed by the ministry. But the gentleman, when he told us this story, should have recollected the oath put to witnesses in the courts of justice—not only to tell the truth—but the whole truth. He should, therefore, have proceeded a little further, and informed us, that the Irish nation having, by a successful struggle about the year 1780, in which they were favoured by the American war, thrown off the yoke of British tyranny, and assumed a situation equal to that of England, they turned their first thoughts to the establishment of a public bank, as congenial with their then situation. Whether or no they have established it, I cannot say positively, having the story only from a newspaper writer, of the gentleman's own side. But this much is certain, that while Ireland was in a state of subjection, she rejected the idea of a bank—but when in our situation, she regarded it as advantageous. Thus this instance, on which the gentleman has dwelt with a great air of triumph, proves nothing in his favour.

Another principle laid down in the report of the committee of the late house, is the incompatibility of the bank and the paper money of government. On this occasion we have had an eulogium on paper money, from governor Pownal. But let it be confidered that paper money is the offspring of credit and confidence, which this state was possessed of before the revolution. Under such circumstances, he spoke highly of its uses: but Pownal would have been both a knave and a madman to contend for it, when both credit and confidence were wanting. An argument has been here made use of, that we have emitted paper money with success. It is true we have made an experiment, and it has not failed. But let us stop here. I am confident that to attempt another

ther emiffion would deftroy that already in circulation : and I would remark that it has owed fome of its credit to the falfe calculations made upon the extent of our revenue. I hope it will maintain the degree of credit it poffeffes. There always have been, and always will be numbers of people in want of money : but if we go on making it, till every body cries hold, we fhall reduce it from being equal to gold or filver, not to be equal to lead. Several ftates which have been wife enough to prohibit paper money among them, have by that means encreafed their fpecie in a great degree.

To conclude : Banks are in general encouraged in all the commercial nations of Europe. And the more republican a country is—or at leaft the greater degree of liberty it poffeffes—the greater is the fuccefs of its banks. Why then fhall our puny politicians pretend to oppofe their fpeculations to the experience of Europe for ages ? A public bank affords many advantages. It on occafion gives aid to government—and fecurity and convenience to individuals. Indeed a certain degree of commerce renders a bank fo abfolutely neceffary, that if this public bank be deftroyed, private banks will arife out of its ruins, 'till the demands of trade are fatisfied. Thefe will not be of fuch governmental utility, nor afford fuch private fecurity. If the laft houfe had this in contemplation, where was their wifdom ?—if not, where was their forefight ?

Mr. Woods fpoke in favour of the report.

Mr. Fitzfimons faid, he wifhed the debate had been confined to the report of the committee : not that he was apprehenfive a general difcuffion would operate againft the refolution recommended in the report : but he wifhed to take the ftatement as made by the committee, and examine whether it was founded or not. The gentlemen in oppofition to it, did not choofe to fight the battle upon that ground.

Here the Speaker declared, that having confidered the queftion as of the greateft importance, he had been willing to allow the utmoft latitude to gentlemen in the debate.

Mr. Smilie was forry the fpeaker's conduct was called in queftion. There had been no juft caufe of complaint. It would have been extremely improper to confine the members to the report. The queftion fhould be taken up on the broadeft ground.

Mr. Fitzfimons declared he had no idea of arraigning the conduct of the fpeaker ; nor did he mean to control any member in his manner of managing his arguments on the
prefent

prefent queftion. He had only expreffed his own wifh that the debate had been confined within a narrower compafs. He then proceeded thus :

I advocate the refolution recommended in the report, and fhall continue fo to do, on this principle, that the late houfe of affembly had not thofe lights, nor that information that could warrant their proceedings. This is the proper fubject of debate: but the gentlemen on the other fide of the queftion, know that it is not their ftrong ground. They therefore abandon it. Neither a corporation nor a citizen can be deprived of any rights without being heard: this is the ground of the refolution now under confideration. But fince the gentlemen have wandered away from this point, I fhall endeavour to follow them on the ground they have taken.

One gentleman fet out with requefting the houfe to confider that the members on this fide of the queftion are pleading their own caufe: and that they are interefted in the inftitution of the bank. I believe I am the only member in this houfe, who have a feat in the direction of the bank. But I fubmit to the houfe whether or no this obfervation is candid. I hope our votes and our conduct in this houfe will not be influenced by any partial interefts which we may have in the inftitution, but by what, in our opinion and judgment, will have a tendency to promote the general good. I have had the honour to be one of the directors of the bank from the firft inftitution of it—and I take upon me to fay, that in no other fituation whatever, could I have been fo ufeful to my fellow-citizens.

In anfwer to the charge made againft the late houfe, of their not hearing the prefident and directors of the bank on the firft application, a gentleman has told us it was in their difcretion whether to hear them or not. The difcretion of the houfe is not eafily defined. But I believe it will be admitted that it fhould be bounded by reafon. And furely it is not confiftent with reafon or juftice to condemn people unheard. I contend that the late affembly acted without either reafon or juftice.

In the courfe of this debate, many affertions have been hazarded, without proofs being brought in fupport of them. Among the number, is that refpecting the terrors and influence of the bank having been exerted to procure figners to the memorials prefented to this houfe in favor of that inftitution. If I were to affirm the contrary, the gentleman who made the affertion, would find it extremely difficult to bring any confirmation of it. I think I have good authority for faying that no fuch terror or influence was ufed. The figners in general are perfons above influence or terror—of independent fortunes and fituations.

The gentleman from Fayette county made a conceffion, which, I think, will operate much againft him. He acknowledged that the charter of the bank was not repealed for any injury received from that inftitution—but from an apprehenfion of what might arife from it. If this be a fufficient ground to warrant the proceedings of the late houfe, I do not know what we may in time proceed to. The gentleman has argued much againft granting monopolies. But how did he learn that the charter of the bank was a monopoly? He has hereby fhewn his ignorance, or fomething worfe.—The charter of that inftitution did not preclude any other perfons from the eftablifhment of another bank. There was therefore no monopoly.

Sufficient notice has already been taken of the gentleman's extract from the journals of the Irifh houfe of commons. I fhall, however, juft remark, that there are in Ireland, many banks—fome fimilar to that in this city—banks of difcount, and banks of depofit. The little trade that country poffeffes, could not be carried on without banks.

Amongft the charges brought againft the bank, is the propofal made by a member of this houfe to mortgage certain revenues of the ftate to that corporation. But as this propofal was made without the knowledge of the prefident and directors, no charge can juftly lie againft them on that account. I muft confefs I do not wifh to fee government attached to that inftitution. It is better to keep it for the benefit and promotion of trade and commerce.

The gentlemen who have fpoken againft the report, feem to think it neceffary to introduce a popular topic, however little connection it has with the fubject under debate. Paper money is fpoken of largely. We are told that the paper money of the ftate cannot exift with the bank. Before they made this very bold affertion, they fhould have known the extent of the emiffion of bank paper : but I dare affirm they could not even form a guefs at its circulation that would not expofe them. I would hazard the proof of this. So much eafier is it to make affertions, than to produce proofs.

Among the charges againft the bank, in the report of laft year, is the interference and threats to reprobate the paper money of the ftate. This charge is founded on the memorial

of

of the committee of merchants, presented to the house while the bill for emitting the paper money was pending. A gentleman has told us that he believes this committee to be all bankers. To what extent this may be founded in fact, I cannot immediately determine. But supposing it true, if, because they hold stock in the bank, they are to be precluded from giving their opinions on public measures, we are in a strange situation indeed. The crown of Great-Britain sometimes dismisses placemen, when they vote contrary to the court. But I did not expect to see a tyranny of this kind established in Pennsylvania.

Another argument I have heard alleged, is, that the officers of the bank were busy at the late election. If being connected in the bank, were to deprive a person of the right of canvassing for his friends, I believe no man would wish to hold a share. No principle can be more destructive to liberty than this.

The gentleman from Fayette county, has expressed surprise that I should differ in opinion, with respect to the balance of trade, from the learned counsel, who pleaded in favor of the bank before the late house. I do not make profession of a very extensive knowledge—but in matters of trade and commerce, I have had some experience, and do not usually commit myself without knowing the ground I stand upon. I should be glad to be informed how the bank can possibly facilitate the exportation of specie. It lends out money at short periods, at the end of which it must be repaid, or the borrower forfeits his credit. Sometimes, through tenderness, the credit is prolonged.—But how this can be said to facilitate a drain of specie, is a mystery to me. What must be the situation of the bank, if that were the consequence of the institution? It must eventually be drained, and if there were not money in the vaults, there must be an end of the bank, and a destruction of the charter, and of all persons concerned. But I assert, that it does not facilitate the export of specie.

The gentleman from Montgomery county (mr. Lollar) has made a curious observation—and many such have been made in the discussion of this business: he has said that the merchant abroad would not so easily procure cash for his goods, were it not for the bank. That the bank enables a man to pay his just debts, is a charge I never expected to hear brought against it in a legislative assembly. It can never be the interest of the state, that her credit should be lost. The support
of

of it tends to promote the advantage of every perfon in the country. Pennfylvania is at prefent, and has been fince its fettlement, indebted to Europe : and that very circumftance, fingular as it may appear, has been highly beneficial. The capitals trufted by the Europeans to people here, have enabled them to build houfes, and to improve the country. Can it then be proper to deftroy that credit ? Surely the legiflature will never fanction fuch a meafure.

I fhall here mention a circumftance, which would have come in with more propriety in another part of my difcourfe. When gentlemen complain of the fcarcity of money, and charge the bank with banifhing the fpecie, they do not know or confider, that, of the ftock of the bank, 360,000 dollars belong to inhabitants of others of the united ftates, or of Europe, and have been brought here merely by means of the bank. So that it clearly appears, that this inftitution, which has been fo frequently and fo unjuftly charged with facilitating a drain of fpecie, has produced an effect directly the contrary.

The dangerous influence of the bank, is a topic much infifted on. This is a mere matter of fpeculation, which it is very difficult to reafon upon. The ftock-holders are about three hundred in number : they have different views and interefts, and are of different parties in politics—it is not likely, therefore, they can ever join in any fingle meafure. How, then, this fo-much-dreaded influence can operate, it is not eafy to conceive. I have already faid that I am the only perfon in the direction of the bank, who have the honor to fill a feat in this houfe : and I fhould hope that if there were no fuch inftitution, my election might be otherwife accounted for.

Mr. R. Morris. After what has been offered by my colleagues againft the report made by the committee laft year, I expected the gentlemen of that committee would have rifen, to vindicate it. But I find the conteft is, who fhall have the laft word. I fhall therefore alter the plan I propofed to follow in this debate, and endeavour to anfwer the objections which have been raifed againft the bank, before I proceed to the confideration of that report.

The firft obfervation made by the gentleman from Fayette county, was, that we on this fide the queftion, are pleading the caufe of our own intereft. This I confider as an appeal to the feelings of the members, and a kind of folicitation to pay little regard to what falls from us, as being parties

ties interested in the decision. This is neither fair nor candid. Every member should have been left to judge for himself, how far interest might influence our sentiments. I acknowledge myself interested in the bank, as a stockholder. But I have no more share in the management, than that gentleman himself, unless when the stockholders are called together. I feel myself interested in the fate of the bank, from another cause. I had some hand in forming the institution, or brat, as it has been called by some of its opponents out of doors—now, so far as I had a hand in the formation of this brat, I esteem myself bound in honour to support it. I am induced also to support the report now before the house, because I have a perfect and thorough conviction, that the institution, in its operation, far from being injurious to the state, is of service to every individual in it. It promotes the grandeur of the state—increases its wealth—and adds to its dignity.

If the argument of our being interested in this question, were allowed the force it was meant to have, the same argument would apply on every question. As a citizen and a freeman, entitled to all the privileges and immunities which the laws and the constitution afford, I am, more or less, interested in the decision of every question that comes before this house. This argument would in effect apply against every member in the house. But I shall quit this ground. As a member of this house, I ask and claim attention. If the arguments I shall make use of, appear to arise from self-interest, they will of course have but little weight: but, if founded on just and equitable principles, I trust the members will be influenced by them as they deserve —and I hope there is no man in this house so determined against the bank, but that he will alter his opinions, if sufficient ground appears to warrant the alteration.

In the opening of this business, I objected to reading the memorial from the president and directors of the bank. It was presented during the last session, at a time when the parties interested in that institution were solicitous to have the matter brought before this house. But during the late recess, there was a meeting of the stockholders, at which it was determined to appeal to the judicial powers---and bring to an issue at law, this question---whether a charter once given, can be annulled, without a forfeiture being proved? This being their resolution, it appeared improper to press the business forward in this house on their part: and it was

agreed

agreed that it should not be resumed here at their instance. However, in the mean time, their fellow-citizens took the matter up; and by their numerous memorials, have put it in the power of the house, to retrieve the dignity of the legislature, by repealing the late act. I, for my part, should have no hesitation to risque the question in the courts of justice. For though some of the judges, in their individual capacity, may have been opposed to the bank, yet I have too much faith both in their integrity and in their regard for their law characters, to believe that they would hazard an unjust decision. Our judges, as judges, are, I trust, upright.

In answering the arguments alleged by the members opposed to the adoption of the report now before the house, I shall endeavour to follow them as well as I can. The member from Montgomery county has told us, he regards the terms of the report, as a declaration of war, and a challenge to all the members of the late house, who have seats in the present. On this point I must beg leave to differ from him. The committee of the former house had been instructed to perform certain duties: the committee of the present house discovered and ascertained that they did not perform those duties, and charged them accordingly with the failure. One of the members of the committee of the late house has, in a great measure, conceded the point, by acknowledging that they did not make the enquiries enjoined; and in justification he tells us, that the house had a right to judge for itself. How then can a censure levelled at the committee for non performance of duty, be construed to extend to those members of that house, who voted in conformity with their report, believing they had performed what had been enjoined them? I should think that those members of the former house, who have seats in the present, by joining in the repeal of the law for taking away the charter of the bank, if they were led to vote for it by a report not founded in fact, would act more honourably and consistently, than by persisting in a defence of that law. If they be convinced that deception has been used, there can be no dishonour in changing their opinions. It was therefore wrong to style the report a declaration of war.

The gentleman went further. He said, if he were to pass reflections on the subject, it should be on that house which granted the charter—not on that which repealed it. I have not examined the minutes of the house which granted it, and therefore cannot tell whether or no he was a member. But I venture

I venture to pronounce, that if he had been, he would have joined in granting it. The neceffities of the country loudly demanded that grant. I prefume he would not pafs his cenfures, but with refpect to the term of the charter— as he appears to think its objectionable part, is the want of limitation as to time, and the great extent of capital the corporation is allowed to poffefs. As to the limitation of time, he tells us, it was not underftood by that houfe which gave the charter, that it was to be for a perpetuity. To confirm this, he produces a claufe propofed as a rider, introduced for the exprefs purpofe of limiting its duration, or to put it in the power of a future houfe to do fo. He adds, that the argument adduced in fupport of the rejection of that rider, was, that the charter muft neceffarily always be within the power of the houfe. But what is all this to us? Are we to regulate our conduct by the private opinions of the members of a former houfe of affembly? On this fubject, I fhall further obferve, that they feem to have changed fides, on this queftion: for the gentlemen oppofed to the bank at that period, were convinced that the houfe could not attempt a repeal or alteration of the charter, unlefs an exprefs claufe was inferted for the purpofe.

Among other objections to the charter of the bank, brought by this gentleman, he alleged that the ftate had received no confideration for it. But this is an affertion which cannot be fupported. The ftate received a very ample confideration. However this is totally out of the queftion. Are we to make fale of our charters? Is there any confideration received for the numerous charters which this houfe is continually granting, and which employ a great proportion of our time? If any is received, I fhould be glad to know who gets the money. But we are not to fet up for fale, charters which the conftitution authorifes us to grant for the good of our country.

The fame gentleman further tells us, he has a ftrong objection to the bank, becaufe it facilitates commerce. From this I prefume he is an enemy to all commerce, and thinks we would be better without it. I wifh the gentleman had favoured us with an explanation of what he meant by facilitating commerce. From what he has faid, I imagine, that explanation would be, that the bank enables people to bring more goods into this country than they otherwife could do, which is difadvantageous. As to the theory of commerce, I do not pretend to be deeply verfed in it: but I have had fome experience

experience in the practical part, and therefore I shall go into a short inveſtigation of the ſtate of our trade, ſince the peace concluded in 1783. At that period, the people of Europe, whoſe attention had been drawn towards us by the arduous ſtruggle we had been engaged in, conceived the moſt flattering golden dreams, with reſpect to this country. After ſo long a war, they imagined we could have no manufactures, and that we were in want of every thing. He that could ſend here quickeſt, it was thought, would the moſt effectually reap the golden harveſt. This occaſioned the immenſe importation of goods which were poured into this country, from all quarters. Goods ſo imported have been ſold at ſuch a great loſs, that the trade has undergone a change and regulation from its own nature: and we ſhall have no more of thoſe wild adventurers coming amongſt us. How the bank facilitated thoſe gentlemen in the management of their buſineſs, I cannot aſcertain. When they ſold their goods, they received for them either money or produce. If they received money, they could certainly ſhip it off without the aſſiſtance of the bank: and if they received produce, they could have no recourſe whatever to the bank. Perhaps the gentleman means, that if the bank had not afforded the facility of procuring caſh for exportation, they would have been glad to take produce. But admitting this for argument ſake, it would make no difference, unleſs he can ſhew that any of our produce has periſhed for want of being taken off our hands.

Another charge made againſt the bank is giving preference to favourites. This is an extraordinary kind of accuſation to be made here. If the ſtockholders, indeed, had cauſe; and were to bring that charge, there might be ſome propriety in it. The money in the bank is the property of the ſtockholders and depoſitors, who have confided the management of it to the directors, with a power to truſt whomſoever they ſhall ſee fit: and the directors are accountable for their conduct to the ſtockholders and depoſitors only. But ſetting this aſide, I maintain that the aſſertion is falſe. When it was made, it ſhould have been proved. I now call upon the gentlemen oppoſed to the bank, to prove the charge of partiality or favoritiſm.

Mr. Lollar ſaid the directors were able to give thoſe preferences ſtated in the report of laſt year. He had not meant to charge them with having done ſo—but to ſtate how much was in their power in that reſpect.

Mr. R. Morris.

Mr. R. Morris. Infinuations are one mode of making charges; and the worst mode: becaufe it is a very difficult matter to difprove them. But I call on any man for proof, and I do not hefitate to affirm that none can be brought, I have fo much confidence in the fidelity of the directors.

The gentleman from Montgomery county, has told us that under the old government, when there were men in the management of affairs as wife as any fince, they had no idea of a bank—and that they fubfifted without it. The old government had no idea of an alliance with France: but this obfervation affords no argument againft either the one or the other. However, though the old government had no idea of a bank, the commercial men of the province had: and I, as a merchant, laid the foundation of one; and eftablifhed a credit in Europe for the purpofe. From the execution of this defign, I was prevented only by the revolution. This affertion, therefore, like many others, is unfounded.

Againft the bank, governor Pownal's eulogium on paper money and a loan office is quoted. I agree that the eftablifhment of a loan office, faithfully and properly conducted, is a wife meafure. But are a loan office and a bank incompatible? No, they are not. A loan office, eftablifhed on proper principles, and on a folid foundation, would promote and encourage the landed intereft, and operate as much in its favour, as a bank does in favour of commerce. The landed and commercial intereft are as nearly allied here as in any country whatfoever. If the country gentlemen are willing, I will freely join in the creation of a capital in hard cafh, for the eftablifhment of a loan office. The interefts of the bank can never interfere with theirs.

But with refpect to a loan office, it feems to be by many affumed as a principle, that it cannot be advantageous without paper money. True it is, it was formerly eftablifhed by means of a paper emiffion. But then the government was in full poffeffion of the confidence of the people: and paper money is the child of confidence—and of confidence alone. That confidence has been deftroyed—and it will require that during a number of years, the fovereign authority be adminiftered with the moft rigid juftice, and the moft punctual compliance with all its engagements, before it can be regained.

It has been afferted that this confidence has been regained: and in fupport of the affertion, we are told that the late emiffion of paper has been fuccefsful. But I pledge myfelf, that

that if one hundred pounds in specie be sent out of this house, there may be procured for it, in less than an hour, 105, but in order to be within bounds, I will say 102½, or 103 pounds, in the paper money of the late emission. This I know to be a fact. Can that, therefore, be said to be money, which is an article of purchase and speculation?

Here I shall make one observation, tho' it seems foreign to my subject: but it has been suggested by the idea of a loan office. I have some share in the landed interest—and hold a large quantity of lands within this state—I am willing to submit to a tax to be paid in hard money, to establish a fund for the purpose of lending sums to farmers for the improvement of their lands. A farthing an acre on all the lands in the state, would soon accumulate into a solid capital fully adequate.

The member from Fayette county, has made an observation, which involves a kind of contradiction in it. He asks with a triumphant air, can the 2947 memorialists in favour of the bank, be said to speak the sense of Pennsylvania? This is very different from the language held forth last year, when 1199 petitioners against the bank, though opposed by 608 in its favour, were said to speak the sense of the state. Now, if 1199, opposed by 608, can at one time convey the sense of the community, 2947, without one person opposed, may, by as fair a construction, be said to convey it at another. I wish the gentleman had amused himself in looking over the names of the signers; he would have seen, that to style them respectable, as is done in the report, was not an error. He has said, this is holding out an aristocratical idea, and that there is no distinction of characters in Pennsylvania. What! is it insisted that there is no distinction of character? The respectability of those signers is not, as he has hinted, confined to property.—Surely persons possessed of knowledge, judgment, information, integrity, and having extensive connections, are not to be classed with persons void of reputation or character—with criminals who infringe the laws, &c. &c.: for such we have amongst us: and if any one doubts it, he has only to cast his eyes to the other side of the state house yard, towards the prison, and his doubts will be removed.

The same gentleman has given it as his opinion, that the number of signers to the memorials, were procured by the influence and terrors of the bank. But this is not founded.

In no inftance was a bufinefs of this kind more fairly conducted. The greater number of the memorials are conceived in one ftyle and form—every member of this houfe muft know that they were publifhed by thofe who formed the defign, in the different newfpapers in the city: fo that every man was able to judge of the contents before he was requefted to fign. Does this favour of undue influence or terror? But what are thofe terrors? When money is fcarce, and people much in want of it, it is a favour to obtain difcounts. The directors have never refufed an enemy of the bank, merely as fuch. Where, then, are thofe terrors? Is it by refufing difcounts to thofe who would not fign, that thofe terrors are to be excited. Look at the memorials, and fee who has not figned them. Few entitled to difcounts are not there. This charge of influence and terror, is not warranted by fact.

The gentleman went into a hiftory of charters in the 13th and 14th centuries; and told us that fome charters were facred, becaufe they fecured the natural rights of mankind: others were not, as being in favour of monopolies. By this, I fuppofe he meant to infinuate that the charter of the bank was a monopoly. I wifh, that inftead of confining himfelf to make this charge, he had endeavoured to fhew how it is a monopoly. If ever there was any room for the charge of monopoly, it was during the war: becaufe it was then recommended by congrefs, that no other bank fhould be eftablifhed, the exclufive operations of this being effentially neceffary to the united ftates.

Whatever weight there might have been in this, during the war, was entirely done away at the peace. But what is this monopoly? A right in the ftockholders to lend their own money to whom they pleafe. Does this hinder any other body of men from doing the fame? If the rights of property are not of the nature of thofe we receive from our creator, yet the fecurity of them is amongft the great objects of civil fociety: and if in a government formed for protection of property, after the bank has been endowed with certain rights, privileges and immunities, thefe are not to be facredly fecured, the very end of government is violated. If there is the difference between charters, ftated by the gentleman, who is to be the judge which are to be held facred, and which not? The conftitution has given no fuch power to the legiflature: It has, indeed, authorifed it to grant them: but not to take them away. Charters in Great Britain are granted by the authority of the king, who cannot

again

again resume them at pleasure. It rests with the courts to determine whether or no they have been forfeited.

In order to justify the conduct of the late house, the gentleman has supposed that the legislature were to grant a monopoly to five men, of our trade to Europe—to five others, of our trade to the East Indies—and to a third five, of our West India trade. But I ask, how can he have recourse to such a vague and idle supposition, or build any argument on it? If any legislature dare violate the most undeniable rights of the community in so flagrant a manner, their acts would be nugatory in themselves. But what rights were invaded by giving the charter of incorporation to the bank? Any set of men might apply for an act of incorporation for the same purpose to the legislature, whose hands were not tied up by the one they had already granted. When a set of gentlemen, opposed to the present bank, and who thought to destroy it, lately applied to the house for a charter for another, the president and corporation of the bank in existence, petitioned against their request. And very properly they did. If any set of men were to apply to the legislature for a charter, which I thought injurious to my private interest, I should, if I had arguments of sufficient weight to offer against it, make an appeal to the representative body.

The gentleman has asked, to what purpose are our annual elections, if a succeeding house has not power to correct the errors and misdoings of a former one? It cannot be denied that they undertake to alter and change the acts of their predecessors—and in consequence, we have had more doing and undoing since the revolution, than ever was known before. This is much to be lamented. It serves to destroy the confidence of the people in the government. The late assembly had no necessity—nor will they ever be justified, for passing the repealing law.—This house, I trust, is disposed to render justice to the injured, by annulling that law. Our constituents have shewn their sense of the late repealing law, by the number of those in favour of it, who have not been re-elected. Wherever a re-election took place, I am persuaded it arose from misrepresentations, by which the electors were deceived: and I venture to pronounce, that, as the utility of the bank comes to be more generally known, and the subject better understood, every member who voted against it, will be discarded by his constituents.

The gentleman frequently gives us little scraps from history; and I give him credit for his reading, which I am always

ways ready to hear, and pay proper attention to, when it bears any analogy to, or runs parallel with the subject in debate. He has brought us an extract from the journals of the Irish house of commons to prove that another people had strong objections to the establishment of a bank. I wish I were deeper read—perhaps had there been no revolution, I should have been so. I have read some history—but I will not trust my memory: On this occasion, however, I shall observe, that in 1721, the period in which the question of a bank was agitated in Ireland, the people of that country were in a situation very different from that of the people of Pennsylvania at present. They were under the government of Great Britain; which held their commerce in trammels. They could hardly pretend to the enjoyment of liberty. This was, moreover, at a time when the public mind was agitated by bubbles of government, which were brought forth, and burst in different parts of Europe. The people, therefore, were afraid of every new scheme. But if the Irish could have established a bank, and had the management of it themselves, they would have had no objection. After their late successful struggles for the recovery of their freedom, I am sure they either have already, or will soon establish a bank among them. But Ireland is a country which does not boast of its wealth or commerce. It is a very good country for importing people, linen, and potatoes from—but I should not have looked to Ireland to import from thence commercial establishments or precedents.

The proposal to mortgage the revenues to the bank, has been held up in a very alarming point of view. But what was the amount of this proposal? Merely that certain revenues should be appropriated to the payment of the interest of debts due by the united states to citizens of this state, and that the revenues devoted to that object should be mortgaged to the bank. What were the terms of that mortgage? That so long as government continued it, the bank should pay the interest punctually when due. Is this, then, the terrible proposition, so fraught with danger to the state? It is, indeed, as strange a construction as ever I heard. And who was this proposition made by? By me, not by directions of the bank—for I had none: not as a stockholder, for I have no authority in their councils: but as a member of the committee of ways and means; in which situation it was not only my right, but my duty, to make a proposition which I esteemed so highly advantageous to the state. In that view
I made

I made it—its fate every body knows—I am apprehenfive that fome will have caufe to lament it. But I hope not. From what I have faid on this matter, it will clearly appear, that the propofition was made by an individual, not authorifed for the purpofe, and therefore fhould not injure the bank.

We are told, that the bank and the paper money of the ftate cannot exift together. But they do exift together. The bank exifts in full credit, although deprived of the countenance of the legiflature: and the gentlemen infift that the paper money is alfo in full credit: This affertion, therefore, is controverted by fact.

The gentleman from Fayette county, appears to be of opinion, that as we have found the paper money profitable, we fhould continue to emit it; and afks, how we could have paid the public creditors laft year without the late emiffion? I anfwer they would have been better paid, if the paper money had not been emitted. It began to iffue from the treafury in July laft, by payments to the public creditors: and during the laft feffion of affembly, in October, or November, nearly the whole of it had found its way back again. The public creditors received it in payment of their demands—they paid their debts with it, or bought what they had occafion for: and it was brought into the treafury—not, I prefume, as a pledge or prefent—but in payment of taxes and impofts, which, had they been paid in proper time, would have lodged the fame amount there in hard money, at leaft as early as the paper was emitted, for payment of the public creditors; and would have prevented the neceffity of an anticipation of thofe public revenues, which were at the time actually due. The paper money was emitted at a very great expence.—The public creditor received it, and was obliged to pafs it at a lefs rate than its value—while the merchant was thereby enabled to pay off his impofts, and the taxable perfon his arrears, with lefs than their amount. How long fhall we go on robbing one part of the community to benefit the other?

The gentleman has fpoken of the circulation of the late emiffion of paper money. This wants fome explanation. The fum emitted was but fmall—and has been paid into the treafury nearly as faft as delivered out. The revenues of the ftate are fufficient to enfure the circulation of fuch a fum. But what fecurity have we that the next houfe of affembly will not iffue another emiffion, and another? The doubts

doubts and fears of this, and of tender laws, deſtroy the confidence of the public. While theſe doubts remain in the minds of the people, the circulation of paper muſt neceſſarily be quick, as no one will riſque the keeping it long by him.

Much has been ſaid of the oppoſition given by the bank to the late emiſſion of paper money. I acknowledge that I gave it oppoſition—but that was before the law paſſed. I defy any perſon to prove I have given it any ſince. Such has been the line of conduct purſued by my friends. Regarding it as a meaſure not calculated for the public good, we thought it our duty to oppoſe it, while there were hopes of preventing it. But afterwards, when the bill had paſſed, we dropped our oppoſition: as it is the duty of good citizens to follow, when they cannot lead.

It has been argued that the bank is prejudicial to agriculture and improvements; that it has been the cauſe of the high rate of intereſt; and that uſury was unknown before its eſtabliſhment. Theſe are very heavy charges indeed—but they are not founded in fact. By what means can the bank injure agriculture? If diſcounts are injurious to it, then, indeed, the bank may be arraigned. But how are diſcounts injurious to agriculture? I ſay they are uſed on many occaſions, for the expreſs purpoſe of encouraging agriculture, if affording to thoſe that want to purchaſe the produce of the country, the means to make ſuch purchaſes, when they could not otherwiſe accompliſh them, be an encouragement. Let us ſuppoſe a ſhip arrives here from the Weſt Indies with a cargo of rum and ſugars, belonging or conſigned to ſome one of our merchants, who has not an opportunity to diſpoſe of thoſe articles immediately. It is prejudicial to have the veſſel detained—yet though he has value in his ſtores, he cannot procure money to purchaſe flour, to load her. In this ſituation, if there be no bank, there is no redreſs. This is by no means ideal. I have frequently experienced it myſelf. The houſe with which I was connected, have often had abundance of goods in their ſtores and magazines, and been unable to procure ſpecie to lade their veſſels. At this criſis, the bank ſteps forward, and if the merchant has evidence of property in his poſſeſſion, he procures credit—purchaſes produce—and ſends off his veſſel. This is the facility the bank gives to commerce. Without it the farmer and merchant would be equally diſtreſſed: the former would have his waggons waiting in Market-ſtreet,

street, and no sale; while the latter would have abundance of rum, mahogany, logwood, dry goods, &c. in his stores, none of which, perhaps, the other would have occasion for. But by means of the bank, the merchant is enabled to purchase, and the farmer to return home.

The high rate of interest has entirely arisen from the distresses of persons in want of money, who either had no credit at the bank, or run through what they had. They were then obliged to make application to usurers, whose enormous demands rose in proportion to the distresses of their victims. Thus has interest mounted from $\frac{1}{4}$ to 2 and 5 per cent. per month. But did the bank take this interest? No. Did it encourage those who took it? No. As fast as they became known, they were refused discounts. Why then charge the institution with what it has a direct tendency to prevent?

The extraordinary profits of the bank, we are told, not only prevent people from purchasing houses, lots and lands, but even induce those who have them, to sell. But surely those extraordinary profits are as much the object of one man as another—and if one wants to sell on that account, who will be found to buy?—I have, however, authority for saying, that the profits of the bank do not exceed, on an average, $7\frac{1}{4}$ or 8 per cent. per annum, which would never be sufficient inducement to hold stock, if there were no other consideration.

"The bank," a gentleman has said, "has not suffered by the loss of its charter. The stockholders," added he, "have already gained enough." To this I answer, that the bank has suffered in the only way in which the assembly of the state could injure it. And if this house restore the charter, they will not restore what the late house took away. It continues to possess, it is true, the confidence of the citizens of Philadelphia—and of the neighbouring states: but before the late attack made on it, it possessed the confidence of the monied men in Europe. This it has in a great measure lost: and this it will find difficult to regain.

On motion ordered, that the further consideration of the report be postponed.

Adjourned.

Eodem Die, P. M.

RESUMED the consideration of the report of the committee, to whom were referred the memorials praying a repeal or suspension of the law annulling the charter of the bank.

Mr. R. Morris. I was in hopes, that after the many arguments made use of on the part of the bank, some of the gentlemen in opposition, would have risen in reply: but I see they are determined to reserve themselves for the last blow; I shall therefore try to provoke an answer, by offering such further arguments as occur to me, on the subject under our consideration.

The bill, which was enacted into a law, by the late house of assembly, repealing the charter of the bank, was brought in, in consequence of a report made by a committee of that house, which had been instructed to enquire and ascertain, whether the charges made by certain petitioners against the bank, were true or not. Knowing that this question would come before the house, I was prepared to ask the members of that committee, whether such enquiry had been made? and if it had, when and where it was made, and what had been the result? But the committee of the present house have saved me that trouble; they have ascertained and stated in the preamble of their report, that no such enquiry was made. The only member of the committee of the late house who has spoken in the present debate, has told us, that even supposing the committee had not made the enquiry, the house might with propriety take up the consideration of their report: by which he has conceded the point as to any enquiries having been made.—The necessary enquiries not having been made, I would ask, how the committee came by the opinion given in their report, "that the bank is in every view incompatible with the public safety?"

Here mr. Gray called mr. Morris to order. He declared he was uneasy to hear the conduct not only of the late house, but of their committee impeached. It was, in his idea, entirely improper, and not the fit mode of conducting the business. He was uninterested in the question, so far as it related to their conduct, having had no hand either in granting or revoking the charter of the bank—but was decidedly of opinion, that if one house undertook to impeach the conduct of another, it would lead into endless difficulties. There was no other tribunal established by the constitution, with the powers necessary for that purpose, than the

council

council of censors. That body would, at a future day, determine on the conduct of the late house of assembly. The member was perfectly out of order.

Mr. R. Morris. I have been called to order very improperly and indecently: the question pending before this house, is, whether or no an act of the former house shall be repealed? How is it possible to discuss this question, without speaking of the conduct of that house? Several other members who have gone before me, have taken the same ground I have proceeded upon, and have arraigned the conduct of the late house and of their committee—they were not called to order: why then am I singled out? Do I not possess the same rights and privileges as other members? The gentleman has not shewn that I was not in order.

Mr. Smilie said, the gentleman from Philadelphia county [mr. Gray] was certainly right. The member had been out of order. He added, that he would venture to say, such a report as that under debate, had never been produced in any assembly. However, he had no objection to a free and full discussion of the conduct of the late house, and of their committee—as, so far from suffering by it—

Here the Speaker interfered. He said on a question of order, there could not be any debate allowed. If the gentleman who had called the member from the city to order, wished to take the sense of the house, he would put the question: otherwise the member must be permitted to proceed without interruption.

Mr. Gray declining to have the sense of the house taken,

Mr. Morris proceeded thus: Had the committee of the late house been charged with neglect of duty, with a view of bringing them to trial before this house, as the gentleman seems to suppose, he would have been right in giving opposition to such proceeding, and I should have joined him; but that is by no means the case. The subject before us, requires an investigation of the conduct of the late house, and that of their committee which made the report, whereon was founded the law for annulling the charter of the bank: respecting their conduct, and on every part of it, I have a right to speak my sentiments, provided they are delivered in a manner not inconsistent with any privileges of this house.

The report made by the said committee, declares, as I said before, "That the bank is in every view incompatible
" with

" with the public safety." I ask was that committee either able or willing to consider the subject in every view? I do not hesitate to pronounce that they were not. Did that committee take a view of the services which the bank had rendered to the united states? I believe they did not; and yet that was one of the points of view in which they ought to have considered it; for when chartered rights are to be destroyed, the matter should really be considered in every point of view. As the committee did not choose to make mention of those services, many of which must have been known to them, I shall, I trust, be excused for giving some little account of them.

In the beginning of the year 1781, the money and credit of the united states were at so low an ebb, that some members of the board of war declared to me, that they had not the means of sending an express to the army. I mention this only as one instance, to shew that distressful state of our finances, which induced congress to make the appointment of a superintendent, which was done in the month of February in that year: and a still stronger proof of our distress will be shewn, by a bare mention, that a motion was, about the time of that appointment, made in congress, by an honourable delegate from the state of Virginia, to authorise general Washington to seize all the provisions that could be found within a circle of twenty miles round his camp. The motion having been submitted to me, as superintendent elect, I requested that it might be withdrawn, and pledged myself to procure, upon my private credit, a supply of four or five thousand barrels of flour, in a short time, for the use of the army; and I was happy enough to succeed in the attempt. The various scenes of distress, and the extreme difficulties which presented themselves to my view at that time, were sufficient to have deterred any man from the acceptance of such an appointment; but, however unequal to the station, the attempt was indispensible. I found it absolutely necessary, previous to the acceptance, to make certain stipulations, as leading to the only possible chance of success: amongst these was that of not being liable to make good the previous engagements taken on account of the united states, well knowing that such demands must soon have run me down—Another stipulation was made with the minister of France, for a credit upon the king's treasury, which was granted in a very limited degree. That minister did not want inclination to go greater lengths; but I have reason to

believe,

believe, that he was limited by inftructions, both as to the fum and terms of the loan; terms which it may be improper for me to mention here, although they would add another proof of our then miferable fituation.

This credit, however, and the confidence repofed in me by the then legiflature of Pennfylvania, laid the foundation for appreciating the paper money of this ftate, and enabled me to feed and move the army during the remainder of the year 1781. I was happy enough to find that affembly difpofed to give every poffible aid to thofe defigns which were then formed for promoting the public fervice. The executive branch of government was equally well difpofed. I have now a gentleman in my eye who then prefided: he knows the applications I was obliged to make; he gave ready compliance as far as he could, and I feel a pleafure in bearing this public teftimony to his exertions at the time.—Under the preffure of thofe difficulties I have mentioned, the idea of a public or national bank fuggefted itfelf, as a meafure that might be extremely ufeful in my attempts to regain for the united ftates, that credit which had been loft. I made the propofal for eftablifhing it to congrefs, which met their approbation. Every one knows the terms on which it was offered to the public: and yet from the month of May, when the propofals were publifhed, until the month of September or October following, there were not more fubfcriptions in the whole, than amounted to about feventy thoufand dollars. During this time, one of his moft chriftian majefty's frigates arrived at Bofton, and brought a remittance in fpecie of about four hundred and feventy thoufand dollars. This fum was brought to Philadelphia, and depofited in the vaults of the bank. I determined from the moment of its arrival, to fubfcribe on behalf of the united ftates, for thofe fhares in the bank which remained vacant; but fuch was the amount of the public expenditures, that, notwithftanding the utmoft care and caution to keep this money, nearly one half of the fum was exhaufted before the inftitution could be organized. In November 1781, the prefident and directors of the bank were elected; they obtained a charter of incorporation from congrefs—and opened the bank for tranfacting bufinefs in January 1782. I fubfcribed the fum then remaining in the treafury, being about 254,000 dollars, into the bank ftock, for account of the united ftates, which became thereby the principal ftockholders. And I fhall now read an extract taken upon this occafion, from " a ftate-
" ment

"ment of the accounts of the united states of America, during the adminiſtration of the ſuperintendent of finance," which was made out and publiſhed before my reſignation, intended for the information of my fellow-citizens, and depoſited in the treaſury office, under an expectation that the books would have been diſtributed or ſold: why they have been with-held from the public eye, I do not know; I meant them for public inveſtigation; and, as the officer concerned, feared none that could be made into my conduct. It lies with thoſe who have with-held the books, to account for it.

This extract ſtates, that on the firſt of April 1782, the united ſtates poſſeſſed ſtock in the bank, to the amount of 252,918 28-90 dollars; and that they were then indebted for money borrowed of the bank, 300,000 dollars, by which it appears, that if this inſtitution had not taken place, the treaſury would have been 50,000 dollars worſe than nothing.

The requiſitions of congreſs, for 8,000,000 of dollars, which were paſſed the preceding November, required no payment from the ſtates until May: and it is well known, that long after that time, they produced no effect: at that period, public credit had gone to wreck; and the enemy built their moſt ſanguine hopes of overcoming us, upon this circumſtance; but at that criſis our credit was reſtored by the bank.

On the firſt of July 1782, the united ſtates held to the amount of 253,000-28-90 dollars in bank ſtock, and were then indebted to the bank 400,000 dollars, which is nearly 150,000 dollars more than the amount of their ſaid ſtock. I am ſenſible that by mentioning theſe tranſactions, I expoſe the preſident and directors of the bank to the only cenſure that can affect them. The then ſtockholders might with ſome appearance of reaſon have complained that they had extended their credit to the united ſtates too far beyond the bounds of diſcretion: but let it be conſidered, that they were told, and truly told, by him that preſided over the finances, that the fate of their country depended very much upon the aſſiſtance required from time to time at their hands. Their deſire to render public ſervice, and their confidence in the aſſurances given repeatedly by that officer, of faithful repayment, will ſurely juſtify them for having riſqued a part of the property confided to them, for the ſecurity of the whole: but, even ſuppoſing any cenſure to lie, how far ſuch cenſure will juſtify the preſent oppoſition of thoſe concerned

cerned in the attack upon the bank, I leave to the decision of every gentleman present. In October 1782, the united states continued, as before, possessed of bank stock for 253,394 58-90 dollars, and indebted 400,000 dollars. Before January 1783, the president and directors growing rather uneasy at this heavy loan, and fearing censure, they called upon me for relief, and I sold out stock of the united states to the amount of 200,000 dollars, and paid 300,000 dollars in part of the debt: so that on the first of January 1783, the united states held stock for 53,394 58-90 dollars, and owed the bank, 100,000 dollars.

On the first of April following, the situation remained the same. By the first of July, I had sold the whole of the bank stock belonging to the united states, and they remained in debt to the bank, 129,800 dollars. On the first of October 1783, this debt was encreased to 164,781: but by the first of January 1784, the united states were discharged of that debt.

The president and directors of the bank had no pledge after the sale of the stock, for the debt of the united states, other than that of the public faith given in proper writings by their officer. During these times of distress and want, the utility of the bank was not confined to the advances made to the superintendent for public service. It was eminently beneficial, by extending discounts to contractors who supplied the army with provisions, and to others concerned in trusting articles necessary for the supplies of the various public departments; sometimes the notes were discounted upon public, and sometimes upon private credit. I have frequently been obliged to take the contractors' notes to me for the sums due to them, and endorse such notes in my private capacity, so that they might obtain discounts on those notes to pay themselves: by these, and such other means as could then be devised, anticipations were effected, until public monies could be collected to discharge the notes. Some members of this house know, and can vouch the truth of this relation; one in particular, who contracted with me for feeding the troops and prisoners at Reading, on very moderate terms, who gave great satisfaction in the execution, got but little profit, but always appeared well pleased with the opportunity of being so far useful to his country. This gentleman must remember these things well.

From the aids given by this institution, the united states were enabled to keep up, feed, and clothe an army, consisting of a larger number of men than they had had in the field before, or than they could have maintained without these aids. This army was, in every point, on a much more respectable footing than formerly, and they kept the enemy at bay.

And shall this institution, from which, not only the united states, but this state, as a member of the union, hath derived such solid advantages, lose all its merit and credit, by the report of a committee of the late house of assembly, stating opinions, unsupported by a single fact? Had the committee called upon me, I would have given them this information, and given it upon oath, if required. Nay, I am even now ready, if necessary, to quit my seat as a member, and appear at the bar of this house, to prove the truths I have advanced.

I now appeal to that gentleman, who has asserted, that this state has received no consideration for the charter granted to the bank, whether her share of services and credit derived from it, was not an ample consideration? Every person who hears me, will, I doubt not, agree that it was. I will not, however, advocate the cause of the bank, merely from past services; but will try to shew, that it may also be useful to the public in time to come.

The report says, the bank has a direct tendency to banish a great part of the specie from this country. From what information the committee derived this knowledge, or whether it was instinctive, I cannot pretend to decide. But I maintain that it has a direct contrary tendency. The money of the stockholders and depositors is drawn into its vortex, and how is it to be got out of their cellars?—The directors will not certainly give it away—they lend it but for short periods, and few of those borrowers would risque a shipment of money which must so soon be repaid. Formerly, when a ship was put up for London, the remitters who wished to ship specie, were obliged, if they had not the money, to cast about for ways and means of obtaining it, either by borrowing or buying of their neighbours and acquaintance, and away it went if they succeeded. At present, under similar circumstances, the remitters are obliged to make application to the bank for discounts: but the directors being interested to obstruct the shipments of money, and knowing those who want discounts for that purpose, they watch them as closely as a cat does a mouse, and refuse such discounts until the ship is gone.

gone. Such refusals may possibly have given rise, in part, to the charge of partiality. The directors, knowing how injurious the exportation of specie is to the operations of the bank, will not lend money for exportation. No considerable sums can be sought after or obtained for this purpose, without their being aware of it; the experience and habits they have acquired in the course of their management, enable them to perceive the approaching evil; and they endeavour to counteract and obstruct it, as soon as discovered. Thus, although they cannot prevent the exportation of specie, they render it far more difficult than it would otherwise be, and consequently the bank has no tendency to banish the specie. The report of last year, therefore, so far as it is grounded on this charge, is grounded on a falsehood.

This report proceeds to tell us, that the bank, after banishing a great part of the specie of the country, collects nearly the whole of the remainder into the hands of the stockholders. How this can come to pass, it is not easy to ascertain. Every six months a dividend is made of the profits of the bank: and if we reflect who are the stockholders, we shall find it most probable that the dividends are devoted to their current expences, for the support of themselves and families, and by that means circulated again amongst the community. At any rate, the stock cannot increase by means of the profits, unless new shares are purchased, which cannot now be done. And if it were to be done, the number of stockholders would increase with the number of shares sold: consequently the charge of accumulating the wealth of the state, into the hands of a few individuals, falls to the ground.

The report goes on to state, "That the accumula-
"tion of enormous wealth in the hands of a society
"who claim perpetual duration, will necessarily produce a
"degree of influence and power, which cannot be en-
"trusted in the hands of any set of men whatsoever,
"without endangering the public safety." How is this accumulation of enormous wealth to take place? If an individual possesses one share in the bank stock, it cannot accumulate: it will always remain one share: for the profits are divided and drawn out half yearly. An increase of the number of stockholders, increases the number of shares; and by experience has been found to reduce those profits. What then is meant by this accumulation? this influence?

They

They are mere bugbears, held out to terrify the ignorant and unfuspecting members of the community.

If, indeed, it is meant, that by the fale of more fhares, the prefident and directors will have the management of more money than while the ftock is confined and fmall, I grant it: and the confequence would be, that they could, with a larger capital, be more ufeful. As to influence, it may be depended upon as a fact, that if ever fuch an inftitution could create influence, this bank has had the opportunity from January 1782, to the prefent time; and who has feen or felt this influence during that period? But fuppofing fuch an influence to exift, how far could it go? it could only extend to thofe who fhould be under a neceffity to borrow; and only fo long as it fhould be confidered a favour to obtain loans. Had this inftitution been let alone, the confidence it had obtained, would foon have procured fuch an increafe of ftockholders and ftock, as would have turned the tables: and inftead of its being deemed a favour to obtain loans at the bank, the directors would have been glad to receive applications for them, from men of proper credit: and as the capital increafed, they would not only have been enabled to accommodate the public more generally, but it might have fo happened, that they would have had it in their power to lend to farmers for the improvement of their lands.

Has any of this much-dreaded influence fhewn itfelf in the legiflature? I anfwer, no. If any member will fay yes, let him fhew when—let him fhew how—let him produce evidence of the fact. But if fuch influence did exift, is it poffible that it could extend beyond the bounds of the city? One of my worthy colleagues and myfelf are ftockholders, and gentlemen affect to fuppofe we are under this influence: this is confidering the matter in the worft point of view. But for the fake of argument, if we admit it for a moment, how far does our influence go? We offer our fentiments on various occafions: we urge reafons and arguments which we, at leaft, think ought to have weight, and to carry conviction. But if thefe arguments are offered againft a certain fyftem of meafures, there are certain gentlemen from the country, who poffefs a kind of magic, which produces much greater effect than our reafoning. We carry very few points againft this magic charm: and with a vote on the queftion, our influence is ended.

The report goes further to say, "That the bank is not "dependent on government." I am very glad it is not; and hope it never will be. The moment it becomes dependent on government, that moment it is destroyed. The confidence of the public is necessary to its existence: and that confidence has been acquired by the punctual compliance with its engagements. Were it under the control of government, the people would withdraw their confidence; and neither stockholders or depositors would be found to trust their money under such control. Gentlemen may say what they please of the credit of government; but the fact is, that such credit is not obtained. Government ought to have credit: and no man wishes more than I do, to see it established, but not through this channel. If government, in the present state of things, could control the funds of the bank, and were to apply them to the use of the state, how should an individual, whose money was taken by such authority, obtain satisfaction? Should he go to law with the state? No; the government has too much power, and he must submit to what it should dictate. But if the president and directors of the bank abuse their trust, and misapply his money, the law is stronger than they are: and the law will give him relief.

The report continues, "The great profits of the bank, "which will daily increase as money grows scarcer, and "which already far exceed the profits of European banks, "have tempted foreigners to vest their money in this bank, "thus to draw from us large sums for interest." The committee might as well have stated, that the profits of a mill increase in proportion to the scarcity of corn, by which it loses the toll, as that the profits of the bank will increase as money grows scarcer: for money is the life and soul of a bank, and as necessary as plenty of corn is to a mill. The first part of this clause has, therefore, no foundation in truth: and as to that part relative to foreigners taking away our specie, in payment of the interest or dividends which will arise on their stock, I am glad of the opportunity of entering into the consideration of it, having heard it frequently urged by sensible men as a grievance, that this country should pay dividends to foreigners, which they consider as a kind of tribute. I shall remark, by the way, that when foreigners place money in the bank for the purchase of stock, it proves that instead of facilitating the export of specie, the institution has a tendency to draw it into this country.

I assert

I assert, that it is the interest of this country to borrow money from abroad, and pay either interest, or bank dividends for the use of it.

Did the first settlers of America bring capitals with them? Some few individuals might: but the generality certainly did not: if they could accomplish the bringing the necessary implements of husbandry, it was doing a great deal. The settlers that have continued to follow the first comers, from that time to this, were in the same way: very few have brought capitals; and yet nearly all have grown rich. How did this happen? It has happened by the use of European capitals. How were these obtained for that use? Not by borrowing money; for they could not, it is true, obtain such loans: if they could, the country would have grown rich much faster. But they borrowed goods. America has risen to opulence by means of the credit she obtained in Europe. The goods so borrowed, or, in other words, bought upon credit, were not procured on the same easy terms, on which money is usually lent. It would have been much better for the traders in America, to borrow money at six, eight, ten per cent. or at any rate of dividend made by the bank, and to have purchased their goods with the ready money so borrowed: for with ready money, those purchases might have been made, ten, fifteen, twenty, and perhaps in some articles, thirty per cent. cheaper than on credit.

It is true, that the merchants in England usually shipped goods on one year's credit, without charging interest for that year. But it has been always said, and in some instances proved upon trials in the courts of law, that the year's interest is amply compensated by the advances put on the real cost of the goods, besides other benefices derived by the English merchant, by means of drawbacks, discounts, &c. &c. And if the American importer cannot pay at the expiration of the twelve months, an interest account commences, and is continued in such manner, that he pays at the rate of compound interest, until the debt is discharged. Under these disadvantages, the credit, obtained in Europe, at a rate of interest equal to fifteen, twenty, or perhaps thirty per cent. has been the foundation of that prosperity which we behold in America. That credit has been extended by the importer to the country shopkeeper; and, through him, to the farmer and mechanic, who being thereby enabled to pursue their labours, have drawn produce from the surface and bowels of the earth, which has not only defrayed the

whole

whole of the coft and charges, but enriched the induftrious. Muft not, then, an inftitution which draws money from Europe for the ufe of our citizens, at the rate of 7 3-4ths or 8 per cent. be extremely beneficial? Could America by means of fuch inftitutions, or by any other means, obtain loans fufficient to enable her to purchafe all the goods wanted from Europe, with ready money, fhe would find a vaft and lafting advantage in it. The plan and utility of a loan office are pretty well underftood—A farmer borrows at that office at the rate of fix per cent. per annum intereft—this enables him to improve his land to the beft advantage: and by well directed induftry, he raifes annually from that land an income exceeding the rate of intereft, which foon enables him to difcharge the debt, and enrich himfelf. In like manner, if we can create a credit in Europe, and borrow at fix, eight, or ten per cent, fo long as fuch loans can be employed to raife an income exceeding the intereft paid, we enrich ourfelves by the difference. The eftablifhment of the bank had created that credit in fome degree: and Pennfylvania, fo long as her citizens can derive a better income from the capitals of Europeans vefted in our bank ftock, than thofe Europeans derive from the dividends, ought to hold out encouragement for an increafe of fuch ftockholders, rather than purfue meafures for diminifhing their fhares.

The report proceeds—" Foreigners will doubtlefs be more
" and more induced to become ftockholders, until the
" time may arrive, when this engine of power may become
" fubject to foreign influence. This country may be agi-
" tated with the politics of European courts, and the good
" people of America reduced once more to a ftate of fub-
" ordination and dependence upon fome one or other
" of the European powers." This conveys a moft extraordinary pofition; that foreigners, by depofiting their money with us, fhall become our enemies, and feek our deftruction; and that thofe who place confidence in us, fhall endeavour to ruin us. I hardly imagine that this can require a ferious anfwer. The contrary propofition is felf-evident. Had we at every court in Europe, perfons fo warmly interefted in our favour as thofe ftockholders muft be, we fhould have warm fupporters in cafe any of thofe courts fhould form hoftile defigns againft us. Nothing can make fuch ftockholders our enemies, but breaking our contracts with them.

The report adds, " at beft, if it were even confined to the hands of Americans, it would be totally deftructive of

that

that equality which ought to prevail in a republic." What equality is here meant? Why did not the committee explain it? Holding more or less shares in the bank cannot destroy it, unless they meant equality in the possession of property. If that was their view, they should first have reported a law, fixing limits to industry—and an agrarian law for making an equal division of property. But I believe those measures would prove as disagreeable to the members of that committee, as to the stockholders of the bank. Each of them, I imagine, possesses more now than would fall to his share on such a division; and there is no reason to suppose, they would be fond of parting with what they hold: for, on the contrary, they are like their neighbours, trying to get more. I may be told, that this is my case—Agreed—I have some property; repeated attempts have been made to deprive me of it—I have not only resisted such attempts successfully, but continue to exert myself in the acquisition of more. Make a division, and that industry ceases.

" We have nothing," the report continues, " in our free and equal government, capable of balancing the influence which the bank must create."

On this point, it is only necessary to mention the late attempt—not to balance—but totally to destroy the bank. I shall therefore make no other appeal, than to the report itself, for the refutation of this assertion.

The report proceeds, " We see nothing, which, in the course of a few years, can prevent the directors of the bank from governing Pennsylvania."

Therefore there is nothing, for if there had been, so wise a committee must have seen it. But did they see any thing that was likely to place the government in their hands? I may safely answer no, for if they had, they would not have failed in that part of their duty—they would have mentioned it in the strongest terms.

Again the report proceeds, " Already the house of assembly, the representatives of the people, have been threatened that the credit of our paper currency will be blasted by the bank."

I ask, who made those threats? Is it in proof that the president and directors of the bank have made them? If they have been so imprudent, let it be shewn, and I agree that they abide the consequences: if such threats have been made by other persons, advocates of the bank, can their conduct be urged as a serious charge against the institution? But

But even supposing such threats to have been made, let us see what has actually been done: The only opposition to the measure of emitting paper money, was made during the time that measure was in agitation: and surely that was the proper time for those who disapproved it, to make their opposition. They did not continue to oppose after the measure was adopted: at least the president and directors of the bank did not. It was not expected of them that they should give hard money in exchange for the paper emission: they could not, without being guilty of a breach of trust: but upon the request of some friends to the paper money, they agreed to receive it on deposit, and to answer the drafts of the depositors, drawn at their own will and pleasure; this was done at some expence, much trouble, and at least so far gave countenance and credit, as to induce many to receive it in payment. In fact, they gave the paper every countenance they consistently could, and probably more than they ought to have done.

"If," concludes the report, "this growing evil continues, we fear the time is not very distant when the bank will be able to dictate to the legislature of Pennsylvania, what laws to pass and what to forbear." I hope the legislature of Pennsylvania will always be composed of men independent in spirit—independent in fortune: whilst this is the case, there is nothing to fear from this bug-a-boo; such men would spurn at all attempts to dictate to the legislature.

But I have already shewn, that no such danger as is here held out, can possibly arise from the bank. So long as the electors of the state take care to return for their representatives, men of sense, integrity, spirit, and property, the people will derive security to their lives, liberties, and property. And although it was, some time since, fashionable with some people to cry out, that men of property should be excluded from any share in the government, yet it will be found, that the public safety consists best with placing the government in the hands of those who contribute to bear its burdens.

I have now gone through the report; and have, I think, proved that it is not founded in truth, supported by facts, nor warranted by any information given to, or obtained by, the committee who made it. Instead of adducing facts, they have stated opinions: and what has been done in consequence? The then house of assembly, in consequence of that report, passed an act for taking away the charter of the bank.

bank. The preamble to that act, states, "That the bank has been found injurious to the state."

It is then no longer a matter of opinion—as stated in the report: but is in the preamble asserted as a matter of fact. I maintain that the assertion is untrue. Desirous to treat the former house with as much decency as the occasion will permit, I refrain from using other epithets, which might with propriety be applied; but the round assertion in the preamble to the act, demands as strong a reply: there was no proof to support that assertion: the committee did not even pretend to any. The house was deceived by the tenor and plausibility of the report; and that committee are culpable.

Will this house, then, suffer to remain enrolled amongst the laws of Pennsylvania, an act, passed under deception, and founded on mere assertion of matter, neither proved nor supported? I hope they will not. I hope this house has too great a regard for the honour of the state, to permit that law to remain unrepealed.

Ordered, that the further consideration of the report be postponed.

Adjourned.

Friday, March 31, 1786, A. M.

RESUMED the consideration of the report of the committee, to whom were referred the memorials praying a repeal or suspension of the law annulling the charter of the bank.

Mr. Whitehill. A great deal has been said on the subject now under consideration of this house, I still remain of my former opinion (for I have heard no reason adduced to convince me of the contrary) that the charter and institution of the bank were totally incompatible with the interest and welfare of Pennsylvania. In that opinion I shall remain, until I hear better reasons offered on the other side of the question.

The report before the house, conveys a number of invidious reflections on the late assembly, and on their committee who made the report relative to the bank. In taking a review of it, I think it will appear those reflections are ill-founded, and unwarranted by fact.

It states, " that the report made to the late house, was " grounded in general notions preconceived, or on the cur-
" rent

" rent popular opinions and speculations, without much
" consideration being bestowed on the special subject; and
" the same may at least be said of the petitions presented
" against the bank:"
And " that the house did not derive from either mem-
" bers of that committee, or the said petitioners, those
" clear lights, which would have been necessary to their de-
" liberations, on so difficult and interesting a subject, and
" which, from the instructions to their committee, they
" seem to have desired."

What is to be supposed the enquiry necessary to be made in this case? or what the lights necessary to the deliberations of the house? Are not those popular opinions, the opinions of the people of the state? And can the house of assembly, the representatives of the people at large, have a surer guide to regulate their conduct, than the opinions of their constituents?

The charge of not affording the president and directors a hearing, is ill founded. Because they were not heard until the third reading of the bill, does it therefore necessarily follow, that they were not heard at all?

The late house is charged with having come to a hasty determination, and broken through the procrastinating forms of proceeding, which were fixed as fences, against the sudden violences of power. This is a wrong statement, and a very unjust insinuation. The repealing act was passed with every usual formality.

Not having made any enquiry at the bank, is stated as very criminal in the committee—But that would have been a very improper place to make any enquiry. Would the president and directors have told us of the partiality or favouritism they might have been guilty of? Would they have told us of any failure in their duty? They would have given us no such information. Would they have told us that the bank was incompatible with the safety or welfare of the state? No such thing. A gentleman from the city [mr. R. Morris] has said that if we had applied to him, he would have given us information—But we might as well apply at the bank as to him—he is deeply interested in the institution.

The committee enquired into the nature of the bank—and its compatibility with the public welfare—and found no such compatibility. It has been asked, how is the bank dangerous—how incompatible with the public welfare? I shall endeavour to shew how. It advances paper on the credit of
the

the money in its vaults, and its loans are confined to 45 days—a period which can never afford any opportunity for the country people to profit by it: as it is impoffible they can come down here every 45 days to renew their obligations. It moreover cramps the credit and circulation of the paper money of the ftate.

I am againft the report as propofing to re-eftablifh the bank on its former charter. [Here mr. Whitehill read that claufe of the charter, which empowered the corporation to have a ftock not exceeding ten millions of dollars—and that which appointed the prefident and directors: he then added:] This ftock of ten millions of dollars was too great an eftate—it afforded too great a liberty to the bank. The prefident and directors were incorporated without the houfe knowing any of their bye laws and regulations. The fame perfons might be prefident and directors all their lives. There would have been no end of the corporation, but by a repeal of their charter, let them exercife their powers how they would.

The late houfe has been charged with a hafty determination in repealing the charter: But the houfe that granted it, was much more hafty in its proceedings: as I fhall fhew. On the 22d of February, 1782, a letter was prefented from the prefident and directors of the bank, praying leave to bring in a bill to incorporate the fubfcribers thereto. The 25th of the fame month, the bill was brought in, and read a firft time: no committee had been appointed to prepare it. The 26th, it was on motion read a fecond time, and ordered to be tranfcribed and printed for public confideration. Thus it appears there was not a fingle day between the firft and fecond reading. The 25th of March, it was read a third time, and ordered to be engroffed. The firft of April it was enacted into a law. All this was in the fame feffion. In this mode was the charter obtained. Time for confideration was not allowed to the public, the bill was gone through with fuch precipitancy. Yet the late houfe is charged with having broke through the procraftinating forms, although the repealing act lay over from the winter feffions to the fall, a period of four or five months. At the fall feffions, counfel was heard for and againft it. The committee could not be charged with having deceived the houfe: for after they had made the report, the matter was fairly argued, as well by the members, as by the counfel.—After all this deliberation—all thefe lights thrown upon the fubject—it may be

safely

safely said, that no business ever was more fairly argued—Why, then, are we charged with hasty measures? The bank does not help the farmer—nor promote the agriculture of the state. If the farmer, who is the strength of the country, be cut off from procuring supplies of money, to enable him to improve his lands, the state must languish. A loan office is the only sure means of encouraging agriculture, and enabling the farmer to bring his produce to market. This cannot be established by hard money, for that is in the vaults of the bank: and while the stockholders can derive 16 per cent from their money, no hopes remain of borrowing at legal interest. The laws have guarded against extortion—but these laws are evaded by the bank. Shall we support this engine of destruction, and enable a few men to take advantage of their wealth, and to stop discounts whenever they please, in times of the greatest distress?

The question at present is, whether the state shall give way to the bank, or the bank give way to the state? For the bank is set up as a party in the state—It has created great disturbance. How often has it been before the house of assembly, taking up the public time, and occasioning a waste of the public money? In 1782—in 1784—in 1785—at our last sessions, and now again. What is the design in all this? Is it the good of the state? Can we believe, if the bank had a tendency to promote the interest of the people, that the state would oppose it? If the gentlemen can shew that it has such a tendency, I shall be happy to join in support of it.

I am not surprised the gentlemen are so solicitous to procure another charter for the bank. While it has no charter, their private circumstances are liable to account for any deficiencies: and how do we know whether they can settle their accounts, and have money enough to pay off their notes? Cannot it go on as a private bank? How many banks in Europe are carried on in that manner? I hope we will not give a monopoly of banking to those gentlemen. It has been denied to be a monopoly.—But when other persons wished to establish a second bank, the president and directors of the present bank had sufficient influence to prevent them from getting a charter. Indeed one of the gentlemen from the city acknowledged that it had been a monopoly during the war.

Mr. R. Morris. I beg leave to explain. I did not say that the bank was a monopoly during the war. I only said that if the charge of monopoly ever had any appearance of foundation, it was during that period.

Mr. Whitehill. I believe it will not be denied to be a monopoly, if it has sufficient influence to make head against all attempts at establishing a similar institution. The gentleman has said, that if we do not repeal the law taking away the charter of the bank, an appeal will be made to the courts of justice. I should have been better pleased that this mode had been tried first, and that the matter had not been bro't before this house.

One part of the report states, that the memorialists may be construed to speak the sense of Pennsylvania. How many are there of them? Two thousand nine hundred and forty seven—of whom 670 are from Lancaster county: although we may safely say, it is probable that not 60 are acquainted with the nature of banks, and the various matters contained in those memorials, and the charges they convey against the late house and committee. There were one thousand petitioners from Lancaster against the erection of the shambles in High-street. This, therefore, as has been already stated, only proves the activity of the persons interested in the bank, in procuring signers to the memorials. With the same activity, I have no doubt, twenty or thirty thousand petitioners might be procured to expunge the bank. Therefore it is wrong to say they speak the sense of the community.

The president and directors of the bank, have not only a separate interest from the state—but also an opposite interest. Their advantage lies in depreciating the paper money of the state—for the more of that is supposed, the less of theirs they can issue. Upon every consideration, therefore, the bank is incompatible with the welfare of the state.

One gentleman has said that the state has done violence to the bank—and that it has suffered more than the house can remedy, even by restoring the charter. The house did not take away any of their property—the charter was not their property. It was a piece of sealed writing, which the house might burn when they pleased. Their property is as safe as it was.

The late house of assembly did not take away the charter of the bank for any crime—nor did they charge the president and directors with having forfeited it. They took up the consideration of the matter upon general principles—they found it would be impossible to establish state paper money while the charter remained. Why then should they destroy

the

the credit of that, which was the only effectual mode that had been discovered for relieving the suffering creditors? But a gentleman lately proposed to have all the paper money called in, in order to make way for the bank.

If charters cannot be repealed, because they are contracts, it affords a great invitation to fraud. A gentleman in enumerating the powers of the house of assembly from the constitution, did not read the whole sentence—at the conclusion of which it is stated that they shall possess all the other necessary powers of a legislature. Charters of public corporations, when not found agreeable to the welfare of the people, may be taken away by the legislature. Two instances of the sort have occurred in this state. One was the charter of the college of Pennsylvania, and the other the charter of the proprietaries.

Mr. Finlay. This question, which has so long engaged the attention of the house, and on the merits of which, gentlemen eminent for discernment, have exercised so much ability, is of such importance in itself, and involves in it such extensive consequences, as to justify my requesting the attention of the house to a few observations which I propose to offer respecting it.

Much has been said respecting the extraordinary reasoning in the preamble of the report under debate, which bears evident marks of the manner in which disappointed avarice chagrins an interested mind. I shall observe, that though the reasoning in the report of the committee of the late house, recommending the passing a law to repeal the charter of the bank, were insufficient or mistaken, yet if sufficient reasons do now exist in the nature of the case, to support the principles thereof, it ought not to be repealed. This proposition is supported by legislative and judicial examples. In appeals from the lower to the higher courts, the question is not— " what were the reasons the lower courts assigned for their " decision?" but " whether was the decision just or not?"— Many examples might be produced, of reports of committees, and preambles of laws, not expressing the true and proper reasons of the respective resolutions or laws. To try all laws by the reasons assigned in their preambles, would be an endless task. Therefore, not to dwell on this, I shall endeavour to prove, that the legislature had a power to repeal the charter of the bank; and that sufficient reasons did exist, to justify the expediency of their doing it.

All governments being instituted for the good of the society

ety to which they belong, the supreme legislative power of every community necessarily possesses a power of repealing every law inimical to the public safety. But the government of Pennsylvania being a democracy, the bank is inconsistent with the bill of rights thereof, which says, that government is not instituted for the emolument of any man, family, or set of men. Therefore, this institution being a monopoly, and having a natural tendency, by affording the means, to promote the spirit of monopolizing, is inconsistent with not only the frame but the spirit of our government. If the legislature may mortgage, or, in other words, charter away portions of either the privileges or powers of the state—if they may incorporate bodies for the sole purposes of gain, with the power of making bye-laws, and of enjoying an emolument of privilege, profit, influence, or power,—and cannot disannul their own deed, and restore to the citizens their right of equal protection, power, privilege, and influence,—the consequence is, that some foolish and wanton assembly may parcel out the commonwealth into little aristocracies, and so overturn the nature of our government without remedy.

This institution is inconsistent with our laws—our habits—our manners.——Our laws and habits countenance long credits, and afford slow methods for recovering debts. They subject our real estates to alienation, and to be sold for debts. They divide our estates, both real and personal, more equally among our heirs, than the laws or habits of any other country I know of. We are too unequal in wealth to render a perfect democracy suitable to our circumstances: yet we are so equal in wealth, power, &c. that we have no counterpoise sufficient to check or control an institution of such vast influence and magnitude. We have no kingly prerogative—no wealthy companies of merchants incorporated—no hereditary nobles, with vastly great estates and numerous dependents—no feudal laws to support family dignity, by keeping landed estates undivided. What security, then, can we purpose to ourselves against the eventual influence of such wealth, conducted under the direction of such a boundless charter?

This charter was for a perpetuity—not subject to change:—In this it was contrary to our constitution, which is liable to change every seven years.

But let us take a more distinct view of the nature of this institution, and of human nature itself. Enormous wealth,

possessed

possessed by individuals, has always had its influence and danger in free states. Thus, even in Rome, where patriotism seems to have pervaded every mind, and all her measures to have been conducted with republican vigour, yet even there, the patricians always had their clients—their dependents—by the assistance of whom they often convulsed the counsels, and distracted the operations of the state, and finally overturned the government itself. But the Romans had no chartered institutions for the sole purposes of gain. They chartered no banks.

Wealth in many hands operates as many checks: for in numberless instances, one wealthy man has a control over another. Every man in the disposal of his own wealth, will act upon his own principles. His virtue, his honour, his sympathy, and generosity, will influence his disposals and designs; and he is in a state of personal responsibility. But when such an unlimited institution is erected with such a capital, for the sole purpose of increasing wealth, it must operate according to its principle; and being in the hands of many, having only one point in view, and being put in trust, the personal responsibility arising from the principles of honour, generosity, &c. can have no place. The special temper of the institution pervades all its operations: and thus, like a snow ball perpetually rolled, it must continually increase its dimensions and influence.

This institution having no principle but that of avarice, which dries and shrivels up all the manly—all the generous feelings of the human soul, will never be varied in its object; and, if continued, will accomplish its end, viz. to engross all the wealth, power, and influence of the state.

The human soul is affected by wealth, in almost all its faculties. It is affected by its present interest, by its expectations, and by its fears. And must not, therefore, every thinking man see what advantage this institution has on the human feelings, above that of wealth held by many individuals? If our wealth is less equal than our kind of government seems to require—and if agrarian laws are unjust in our present situation, how absurd must it be for government to lend its special aid in so partial a manner, to wealth, to give it that additional force and spring, which it must derive from an almost unlimited charter? Can any gentleman avoid seeing this to be eventually and effectually overturning our government? Democracy must fall before it. Wealth is its foundation, and gain its object and design.

Thus

Thus it appears that this institution is inconsistent with our general laws, customs, and circumstances, and even with the nature of our government. The proofs are not founded on facts of doubtful credibility. They are drawn from the nature of things: and the principles of nature being justly stated, this kind of arguments are conclusive. They carry their evidence with them, with a certainty like that of the sparks flying upwards, or the waters running to the sea.

Upon the same principles, it is evident that in the present state of our commerce, the bank facilitates both public and private ruin. The balance of trade being constantly against us, commerce with us has contracted a different meaning from what it has in Europe. There it is founded on the produce and manufactures of the respective countries, for which the merchant finds a foreign market, and in lieu of which he brings a suitable return. From the excess of the exports, the nation is enriched. With us it may, with more propriety, be styled importation than commerce: and this importation, carried on to too great a degree before the revolution, is greatly facilitated by the bank.

A worthy gentleman from the city [mr. Morris] has declared it as his opinion, that precedents from Ireland are improper, as that country does not boast of its commerce or wealth, and is under English trammels. He says it is a good country to import people, linen, and potatoes from—but not commercial precedents. I do not pretend to much commermercial knowledge. I have indeed some general knowledge; and am of opinion, if we had such linen and cambric manufactures as the Irish—if we exported so much beef, butter, and pork—and manufactured so much woollens as they do—we should be possessed of the immediate means of commerce. But, being under British trammels, her people, who ought to be employed at home, are obliged to emigrate in abundance. If they are esteemed an article of commerce, that branch of her trade has been much to our advantage.

But as for us, though we have the foundations of commerce, we have not, nor can we soon have the means of carrying it on extensively to advantage. We export flour, which, through the scarcity of labourers, has failed in the quantity. We export flaxseed, which, through the oldness of the lands contiguous to market, and the change of seasons, has also failed greatly, so as to be scarcely worth mentioning. We export lumber, which has failed in like manner, and must continue to fail, in proportion as our woodland is cleared. Is this a balance for our amazing importations, not only from Europe but both the Indies? From those vast importations, the number of our dealing people was increased. The bank gave the means of purchasing foreign cargoes—the accefs was eafy—but the credit fhort.—The hafty day of payment approached—hence the numerous tribe of brokers arofe. The involved debtor went from friend to friend for the affiftance of credit—from broker to broker for coftly fupplies of cafh—until ruin overwhelmed him with confufion and woe: and he who was, or appeared to be, a capital dealer, fell. Like a mighty oak in the woods, he crufhed many by his fall. Thus of late, the cry of private ruin in this city, has not only been heard by our fifter ftates—but by foreign nations. Thus hath the ftate been drained of what money was circulating within it, and the means of fupporting the revenues and credit thereof been taken away: no doubt there has been a concurrence of other caufes. The imprudence of the unfortunate is often affigned as one caufe: and no doubt it was: but experience forbids to fet down the unfortunate always as fools or knaves. Many who had fair and honeft profpects, or who affifted with their credit thofe who had, finding every ufual means of extricating themfelves cut off by the inundation of foreign goods, have, whilft poffeffed of honeft principles and competent fagacity, funk in the common ruin.

Much has been faid of the merits of the bank in preventing the money from leaving the country. I know the exportation of money is contrary to its intereft. But the little arts of the directors, to detain it in the country, are contemptible as an argument, and ineffectual as a means. What are the methods by which they retain it? A gentleman [mr. Morris] has told us, that when a veffel is up for England, the directors know thofe who apply for difcounts, in order to fend the money away, as readily as a cat knows a moufe, and that they refufe them.—Are thefe the mighty means? Is this the boafted fecurity?

I have already proved that the bank facilitates importation: confequently it facilitates contracting debts abroad: and if the debts are facilitated, why clog the payment? Better that the remittances could be made in an air balloon, and the freight faved. In Spain where they have the precious metals poured in from their fettlements, and are manufacturers of money—in order to prevent its being exported, ten

per

per cent. (if I am not miſtaken) is charged on the remittances to England: and a higher duty is charged on the remittances from the Havannah and New Orleans. Yet can any man of underſtanding ſay that the Spaniſh dominions are enriched by this? By no means. They are ſcarcer of money, in proportion to their uſes, than we are.

The way for individuals or nations to get rich, is not to have artificial difficulties laid in the way of paying their debts; but to contract few of them. The debts muſt be paid: and the bank collects the money to a point, where it can be eaſier found in large ſums for exportation, than in any other manner: and thoſe little ſhifts, which depend on perſonal ſagacity or integrity, are fit only for a plauſible colouring for refuſing to ſupply thoſe who are not favourites; and the more effectually diſcover how well it is calculated to promote the monopolizing of trade. What ſecurity have we that its aſſiſtance will not be partially exerted for this purpoſe?

This inſtitution is itſelf a monopoly—being incorporated a great trading company—and having a right to turn ten millions of dollars into trade, if the preſident and directors pleaſe—or to lay out that amount upon land. So, by taking advantage of a ſcarcity of money, which they have it ſo much in their power to occaſion, they may become ſole lords of the ſoil. If they may monopolize trade—if they may monopolize the ſoil—why not the government too? Doubtleſs they may.

I do not ſay whether or no the bank is a monopoly in the ſtrict legal ſenſe of the word. This is not to my purpoſe. But I ſay that it is, in its nature and principles, in the common popular ſenſe, a monopoly: and being ſo in its nature, it muſt be ſo in its effects. This is a certain concluſion. I do not charge the directors or ſtock-holders perſonally with ſuch deſigns: but this being the nature of the inſtitution, it becomes the indiſpenſible duty of the directors to conduct it according to its natural principles.

Great wealth ſeems, even with individuals, to have a tendency to monopolizing. It was the ſaying of a wiſe writer, when riches increaſe, they are increaſed that have them—increaſed in their appetite for riches, and in their endeavours to procure them.

This inſtitution I believe to be inimical to the emiſſion and credit of paper money. Let us for a moment compare the ſtate paper with that of the bank, with reſpect to their ſervice to this country. For this purpose, I beg leave to advert a little to the history of paper money. Its amazing usefulness to Pennsylvania, before the revolution, is well known. But when the necessities of congress obliged them to emit paper money, they were obliged to emit it in great quantities, and had not the power or means of appropriating sufficient funds for its redemption. And to look back, I rather wonder that those emissions served us so well, than otherwise. Though the measure was then unavoidable, I must observe there is not sufficient safety in one public body judging of the quantity of money to be emitted—and another, or rather many other public bodies having to judge of and appropriate the means of redeeming it. But there is more safety in one body being obliged to judge of the quantity—the uses—the funds—and the manner of redemption.

When this state emitted the island state money, as it was called, the funds were sufficient, but not immediately productive; and there was abundance of paper money in circulation. Yet it stood its ground tolerably, until the vast sum of 500,000l. was emitted upon funds uncertain in their operation, and not productive then, nor in a sufficient degree yet. This sunk the credit of the other with it; and became a valuable speculation—perhaps to some of the planners of the emission. The other resumed its credit instantly, when the funds became productive. But having spoken largely on this subject in the last house, I shall say no further now—but observe that the last emission has funds much more than sufficient. These funds are constantly productive; and the uses which keep it in circulation, are abundant. Therefore it cannot fail of holding its credit—and has stood its ground against a very powerful opposition indeed. Though I do not say that any direct attack was made upon it by the directors of the bank—as I do not blame them for not receiving it—yet it was evidently opposed through the influence of that institution. In the eighth general assembly, the directors wrote to the house, dissuading them from the emission they were about to make, giving their opinion that it would not do, and offering a loan. The prophecying its fate, by those who were supposed to have the power to blast it, had the desired effect; and the emission was dropped. When the funding bill was going through the late house, could those who were interested in, or dependent on, the bank, do more than they did, to prevent the emission, and to discourage the people, already rendered suspicious by former events?

Did

Did not the friends of the bank, in that houſe, predict that it would be three or four for one, as ſoon as emitted? Did not the gentlemen of this houſe who are intereſted in the bank, endeavour at our laſt ſeſſion, to have it all called in? Have they not afterwards complained of its not purchaſing the neceſſaries of life? Did not one gentleman tell us it was from two and a half to five per cent. below par? I muſt anſwer, that inſtances of the kind have not ſtruck my obſervation. I very lately changed a conſiderable ſum, and have ſeen others do the ſame, without aſking or being offered any advance. There can be none who would aſk or give any advance, but ſuch as are intereſted in, or indebted to, the bank. At leaſt, in all my dealings in the city, none have heſitated to take it, but thoſe who told me they muſt have money for the bank. Conſidering theſe things, there is nothing wonderful in ſome inſtances of ſuch an advance being given. It is but the price of convenience. I have frequently ſeen three pence given in Ireland for getting ſilver for a guinea: but the people there never thought the gold of leſs value on that account. Many ſuch inſtances might be produced.

A gentleman from the city [mr. Morris] has mentioned the quick circulation of the paper as an argument againſt its credit. He ſays it returns to the treaſury almoſt as faſt as iſſued. I congratulate the ſtate of Pennſylvania upon the news, as a ſatisfactory evidence of returning confidence. It brightens our proſpects of proſperous days. The public creditor has been relieved by it. The moneyleſs farmer has with it paid his taxes, which had accumulated for years paſt. It has brought into circulation the little hard money that remained. Our treaſury is kept buſy receiving it, and as buſy paying it away. Who refuſes the paper money from us? None—for the comptroller general is kept employed almoſt night and day—people hurry him ſo that they may get it. Certainly the gentleman could not mean this as an argument againſt paper money.

Much might be ſaid on the advantages of the loan office. But the principles of this inſtitution are ſo well underſtood, that I ſhould eſteem it an inſult to the good ſenſe of the houſe to enter on them.

Thus far I have moſtly confined myſelf to principles, and the reaſon and nature of things: arguments of this kind being juſtly laid, I take to be moſt convincing: for every man knows things will operate according to their nature.

But

But I beg leave now to animadvert on certain arguments made use of by some of the reasoners on the other side: for hitherto I have only touched on a few of them, in order to illustrate my subject. I would first observe that I took no notes at the time of the debate—as I did not then design to enter so largely on the subject. I shall therefore remark on but few of the gentlemen's arguments.

A worthy gentleman from the city [mr. Fitzsimons] informs us, that he is a stockholder in, and director of, the bank; and that there are several stockholders members of this house.—He justly observes, that this does not debar them from the constitutional right of canvassing for offices at elections—and advocating their own cause on the floor of this house. Doubtless the gentleman is right. For though the constitution excludes executive officers from seats in the legislature, lest they should influence it to make their salaries more lucrative, or their duties more easy: yet the convention neglected to guard against men, who have procured peculiar privileges by obtaining partial laws in their own favour, for the sole purpose of gain, advocating their own cause by the advantage of a seat in this house. This reminds me of the famous laws of Solon, which, though an excellent system, neglected to provide any punishment for a person who should murder his father or mother—doubtless not expecting such a crime would ever be committed. And indeed I think the convention guarded so well against the legislature of this state granting any kind of monopolies, or partial prerogatives, as cut off the probability of any such thing happening in this state: yet such is the course of affairs, that advantage has been taken of the embarrassments and inexperience of the state, and this very thing has happened.

As to canvassing at elections, I apprehend it is not common nor honourable to canvas for a seat in the legislature, where the candidate has only in view to serve the public. But where he has a cause of his own to advocate, interest will dictate the propriety of canvassing for a seat. Indeed the emolument arising from it, would induce but few wise men to canvas for a seat in this house purely to serve the public: for few who know the importance of the service, will think themselves fit for it. We also allow to the gentlemen that they have a right to advocate their own cause, on the floor of this house. But they will allow us to consider, that it is their own cause they are advocating; and to give

give credit to their opinions, and to think of their votes accordingly. And here I call the attention of the house for a moment, to confider the fituation of the parties engaged in this argument: If the bank is a common good—diffufing beneficial influences through the whole ftate—increafing the price of lands and produce—if we faw it to be ufeful to the commonwealth—would it not be our own intereft to encourage it? Can this houfe fuppofe us wicked enough to deftroy our own intereft or the public's from mere envy? On the other hand, this houfe muft obferve, that however hurtful and dangerous it is to the general good, the gentlemen on the other fide are interefted in fupporting it; and if it were fafe and beneficial, it would alfo be our intereft to fupport it.

The fame worthy gentleman has told us, that the circulation and amount of the bank paper is little underftood. This I believe is perfectly true. But is this a reafon that we fhould grant a charter to the bank? Surely not. Shall the legiflature of Pennfylvania enact a charter for an inftitution they do not underftand? Certainly every honeft member on this floor, who does not fully underftand the myftery of banking, or who has a doubt upon his mind, of the fafety or utility of fuch an inftitution, will vote againft the refolution.

Another worthy gentleman [mr. Morris] has told us, that it is his opinion, if the queftion is to come before a court of juftice, the judges, though their opinions might be otherwife, yet on account of their characters as law officers, would condemn the repealing law, as a nullity. What! would the judges complement the bank by deciding contrary, not only to their own fentiments, but to law itfelf? If this be the cafe, it muft be a very influencing inftitution, and a very dangerous one indeed.

The fame worthy gentleman informs us, that if the bank is not continued, there will not, at fome feafons, be a fhip loaded with flour, at the port of Philadelphia. But I afk, how were they loaded before the war? how were they, or how are they, loaded at Baltimore and other ports? Baltimore exports more in proportion to its imports than Philadelphia does: and this is worthy of our obfervation. But as I have detained the houfe longer than I defigned, and as the gentleman who fpoke laft, difcuffed to advantage many arguments I had in view, I fhall conclude by offering a few more general obfervations.

There

There is now no chartered bank exifting: therefore the cafe is before us on original ground. The queftion is not whether or no we will repeal a charter; but whether or no we will give one. Whether or no the laft houfe affigned proper reafons for what they did, is not our bufinefs: for we know they did no injuftice to the bank. They took away none of the property. The holders have their money; therefore it was not like an agrarian law, as the gentleman alleged—They may ftill keep a private bank. And here I beg leave to remark, that as a private bank is all the conftitution admits of, fo it would have the fame advantages in trade, and more fecurity to the people than a chartered bank. For, under the charter, the incorporated property was the only fecurity to the public: therefore the ftockholders, who have the property of it, and draw the dividends from it, might be rolling in wealth, and the bank break and ruin thoufands. The bank might be robbed, or thrown into the Delaware, and the owners who profit by it, be fafe as to their eftates. None but men of wealth have money to fpare to be bankers: and fhall this houfe give a fpecial law to enable monied people to increafe their gain, without having either their perfons or eftates upon the fame level of refponfibility as the other citizens? By no means: this houfe will not do it. If the legiflature did fo, it would give a legal fanction to a fnare of the greateft danger.

This is the only ftate in the union faddled with a bank. Our fifter ftates, fenfible of the magnitude and danger of fuch an inftitution, have, as far as I am informed, refufed to fanction it. Maryland and New York, I know, have done fo. They have feen the danger, and learned by our example. Let us for fome time learn by theirs. Such an inftitution might in time be formidable to the whole united ftates.

I chearfully acknowledge, however, the great merit of the worthy gentleman who has informed us that he laid the plan of the bank, and led it into operations. I acknowledge that the bank has been of great fervice to the united ftates —not in our darkeft times—for thefe were in fome meafure over, when Cornwallis was taken—which was before the bank exifted. But the fervice was reciprocal. It was part of the French money, to the value of which the united ftates became ftockholders, that enabled the bank to open its operations: and if that inftitution was, for a part of the next feafon, of effential fervice, it was but a fuitable return: and the financier, for making fo proper a ufe of it, deferves

and

and enjoys great credit. But the public are not indebted to this inftitution—or, if they are, they will doubtlefs give that debt a preference to debts even much earlier contracted. Congrefs money did us effential fervice in our darkeft hours : fhall it, therefore, be continued ? No : it became dangerous ; and confequently ceafed. The army were no longer neceffary, and would have been dangerous ; and were therefore difcontinued. General Wafhington, with all the virtue and glory of his perfevering fervices, refigned his honours and authority, when he ceafed to be neceffary—though he did not ceafe to be either ufeful or fafe. If we muft be faddled with this dangerous inftitution for ever, becaufe of its former ufefulnefs and conveniency, furely Oliver Cromwell fhould have been rewarded in England by the continuing his heirs to occupy the government, inftead of being branded as a ufurper, and " damned to everlafting fame." By the fame rule, defpotic government, which is the moft convenient, ought always to be preferred and continued.

One other obfervation occurs to me, which I have often thought of, and to which I yet requeft the attention of the houfe. If a bank is fupported in Philadelphia, it will give another kind of credit, and another kind of circulating medium to the city and its vicinity, than to the more remote parts of this extended ftate : and the bank may increafe the circulating medium to any quantity it pleafes, which will occafion an artificial increafe in the prices of things, and the manner of living. It will gradually affect the interefts, manners, and habits, with fuch diftinguifhing peculiarities, as will occafion fooner or later a diffolution or feparation of this ftate. This would be a very undefirable event : and yet the inftituting a bank can fcarcely fail producing it. Perhaps, when this event takes place, this city and a fmall territory around it, may, like Hamburgh and Dantzick, not only promote monopolies, but have its foundation placed in the principles of monopoly and ariftocracy. For the common intereft of Pennfylvania, for the honour and advantage of human nature, I wifh fuch events may be at a great diftance.

Mr. Fitzfimons. The gentleman has mis-ftated fome of the obfervations I made. I did not fay I had canvaffed for my own feat : that is not the truth. Whether my feat is more beneficial to me, than that gentleman's to him, I leave the houfe to judge.

Mr. Lollar. I beg to detain the houfe a few minutes. A
gentleman

gentleman from the city [mr. R. Morris] has been a little facetious in his remarks on some of the arguments I made use of on Wednesday. I confess his superior knowledge, and do not pretend to oppose mine to his. However, when a matter amounts to a self-evident proposition, I think myself qualified to form an opinion on it. I said that the bank facilitated commerce—which, in the present state of our trade was against it, as it enabled the British creditor to carry off cash for his goods, and saddle the merchant here with the payment, in the hasty manner prescribed by the bank. from this he drew an inference, that I was opposed to the payment of our debts—which is by no means the case. With respect to partiality or favouritism, I did not charge the directors with it—I only read part of the petition from Chester county, presented to the late house against the bank, to evince how much was in their power. I said that under the old government, they had no idea of a bank. To this the gentleman answers, by telling us he, at that time, had one in contemplation. I do not doubt the fertility of the gentleman's imagination. He is certainly competent to the forming that or any similar plan : and probably the present bank is the very one he had then in view.

I do not pretend to call in question the usefulness of the bank during the war. The officers and soldiers of our army were likewise useful during the war : but would we infer from thence that they should be still kept up ? The profits of the bank have well paid for its services. Our officers and soldiers have been dismissed with a commutation of pay for five years.

The gentleman tells us, that if the legislature were to grant a monopoly of particular branches of our trade to any set of men, the laws granting such monopoly, would be void in themselves ; and seems to think that the law annulling the charter of the bank, is a nullity—If that be the case, the incorporating law was equally a nullity.

Another member from the city tells us, he has had the honour of being a director of the bank since its first establishment. He might have added, that so he would remain during life, if the present mode of voting according to property, continued. In the bank of England, (if I am rightly informed) every person possessed of a share of 500l. has a vote ; and those possessed of a number of shares, no more.

When another bank was attempted to be established in this city, the president and directors, by lowering their

terms,

terms, drew it into their vortex: and thus defeated the attempt.

The bank is not compatible with our constitution, which does not admit of granting peculiar privileges to any body of men.

On motion ordered that the further consideration of the report be postponed.

Adjourned till three o'clock in the afternoon.

Eodem Die, P. M.

RESUMED the consideration of the report, &c.

Mr. R. Morris. The gentlemen from the country, by fixing such short adjournments, make this a hard service. They scarcely allow us time to take a comfortable dinner and glass of wine, before we are obliged to return to the charge: however, though they are impatient to return home, they should allow us time to consider and digest the arguments used upon this floor. It would be but decent to do so. I shall now endeavour to follow and discuss the arguments of those gentlemen who have spoken against the bank in the present debate: many of them I consider as totally unnecessary; and such I mean to pass by unnoticed.

The gentleman from Cumberland began his oration by telling us, that he still retained his own opinion; and should continue to do so, until he heard better reasons than those yet offered. I never heard any declaration from that gentleman's lips, which obtained more credit with me than this. I do sincerely believe, that he does and will retain his opinion. Even were an angel from heaven sent with proper arguments to convince him of his error, it would make no alteration with him. I did not—I could not entertain the least expectation that my colleagues or myself should be able to produce any effect upon so predetermined a mind as his.

This gentleman went into a discussion of the report now before us, in which I do not mean to follow him. The committee who brought in that report, have justified it: and I have already given it all the support which to me appears necessary.

He has admitted that the committee of the late house made no enquiries respecting the bank, although they were directed to do so: and seems to insist that such enquiries were unnecessary, because the popular opinions, he says, were against the bank. But where did he collect the popu-

lar

lar opinions? How were such opinions communicated? Had he, indeed, said that the opinion of a party was againſt it, he would have ſaid right. But was the popular opinion communicated by 1199 petitioners, even when oppoſed by upwards of 600 remonſtrants? According to the doctrine of another gentleman on his ſide of the queſtion, near 3000 petitioners (unoppoſed) do not at this time convey the popular opinion. But even if we ſuppoſe the late houſe to have been poſſeſſed of the popular opinion, I deny that this was proper ground, on which to found legiſlative acts: nor can it warrant or juſtify the proceedings of the late aſſembly with regard to the bank. Popular opinions originate with individuals; falſe appearances are frequently given by thoſe who have ſecret deſigns: and men for the moſt part take them on truſt. Specious arguments and groundleſs aſſertions take place of reaſon; and run away with what is called popular opinions. The conduct of an aſſembly founded upon ſuch opinions, will not ſupport itſelf. If our laws are to be enacted in conformity with popular opinions, they muſt be altered as ſuch opinions change, which generally happens every two or three months: for opinions, taken up haſtily, and propagated for party purpoſes, cannot hold long. If, indeed, a popular opinion appears to have reaſon and juſtice for its baſis, then it is well to make it the ground of our proceedings. But who is to judge? The repreſentatives of the people: and when popular opinions run counter to reaſon, they ſhould counteract their influence, by ſhewing them to be wrong, and not paſs acts in compliance with them.

The gentleman complains, that the committee of the late houſe have been cenſured for not calling at the bank—laying great ſtreſs upon—" calling at." If that committee thought it inconſiſtent with their dignity to call at the bank, they might have obtained the neceſſary information without calling there. The preſident and directors would have waited upon that committee as readily as they have done on the committee of this houſe; and would have anſwered ſuch queſtions as they might have thought proper to put to them. But he aſks, " of what uſe would it have been, to make enquiry at the bank? Would the preſident and directors have made anſwer to criminate themſelves? Would they have told us that the inſtitution was dangerous to the welfare of the ſtate?" To this I anſwer, that had proper queſtions been aſked, proper anſwers might have been obtained: and although

though the prefident and directors would not criminate themſelves, yet we know, that, in the examination of witneſſes, truth is frequently diſcovered, even when endeavours are made to conceal it. But, in this caſe, there could have been no cauſe of concealment.

I have mentioned in the courſe of this debate, that had the committee called upon me, I ſhould have given them, (and upon oath if required) the ſame information reſpecting the ſervices derived by the united ſtates from the bank, as I have had the honour to relate to this houſe. The gentleman aſks, why apply to me, who would have given the ſame kind of anſwers as the preſident and directors? Let us examine the force of this reaſoning. I am no otherwiſe intereſted in the bank, than as a ſtockholder; and my bank ſtock is more eaſily diſpoſed of, or parted with, than any other of my property, except caſh. Suppoſe, then, that inclination, neceſſity, or any other circumſtance, ſhould happen to induce me to ſell my ſtock, from that moment I ceaſe to be immediately or perſonally intereſted in that inſtitution. But this is not the caſe with me as a member of the community. My landed eſtate—my family—and likewiſe the intereſt I hold in common with other citizens—muſt attach me too ſtrongly to the general welfare of the ſtate, to admit of a poſſibility that I ſhould engage in the ſupport of an inſtitution incompatible with the public ſafety. Should I ſell my ſtock, the purchaſer becomes intereſted in the ſupport of the inſtitution, inſtead of my being ſo: and in that caſe, I ſhould be no otherwiſe concerned in its ſupport, than as a citizen believing it to be of general benefit: and as ſuch, I am perſuaded that I ſhould be as ſolicitous as I am at preſent. The gentlemen oppoſed to the bank conſtantly hold out the idea, that the perſons intereſted in it, are always the ſame—and that it is a monopoly confined to a few. Now it is certain, that on the contrary, the property in bank ſtock is conſtantly changing hands. Where, then, is this permanent intereſt that ſhould induce us to ſacrifice the good of the country to the good of that eſtabliſhment? The market is conſtantly open for the ſale and purchaſe of this bank ſtock: and if the gentlemen in oppoſition ſeriouſly believe in the advantages which they ſay are derived from holding that ſtock, why do they not inveſt ſome part of their property in it—for property they have—and there are always ſhares to be ſold?

The holders of that ſtock differ as widely, I preſume, in their political principles, views, purſuits and deſires, as the

holders

holders of lands, houses, or other property. These gentlemen may, when they please, be of the number. How, then, is this cry of monopoly supported? My information is not to be trusted, because I am interested in the bank: but surely I am more deeply interested in the state—and that in a way too that it is hardly possible for me to detach myself from it, were I so inclined. But very different is my situation with respect to the bank. I am as deeply concerned to obtain good laws, and to enforce the due execution of them, as any gentleman in this house: and I hope, notwithstanding the insinuation made, that it will never be supposed I would sacrifice the interest and welfare of the state to any interest I can possibly hold in the bank.

Such of the members of this house, as are disposed to give a fair and candid discussion to the arguments used in this debate, will see clearly that the bank is neither dangerous to, nor incompatible with, the welfare of the state: and these were the assumed principles upon which the repealing law was founded. If that assumption was taken up lightly and upon false grounds, as my reasoning tends to prove, I hope gentlemen will give that reasoning its just weight: for I cannot see why it should lose its force, on the supposition of my being interested in the event. Let the arguments used, be considered, not as coming from parties interested, but abstractedly as to their force and solidity.

The gentleman tells us, that the bank issues paper on the credit of the money in its vaults—and that its discounts being confined to forty-five days, the farmer can derive no benefit from such limited loans. If the state will deposit hard money in the hands of the treasurer, for the purpose of exchanging it on demand for the paper they may issue on the credit of such deposits, no doubt can be entertained but the state paper, under such circumstances, will have full credit.

In the notes which I have taken of the speeches of my opponents, I so frequently meet with paper money—paper money—paper money—that it will be impracticable for me to follow them throughout on that topic, and speak to it as often as they have done. I find, however, this is the great sore; and cannot help expressing my astonishment at this constant cry for paper money by the country gentlemen, when it is notorious that they will not sell the produce of their farms for it. No merchant, with ever so much paper money at command, can purchase the produce of the country

try for exportation. Therefore I cannot afcribe this conflant clamour about paper money to any other caufe than a defire to pay debts with lefs than their juft amount, or to purchafe lands at lefs than their value. I infift that there is no neceffity for paper money. No induftrious man, in his individual capacity, can feel a want of it : and wherever it is emitted, it will be more likely to produce public mifchief than public good. This queftion of paper money has been agitated in feveral of the ftates ; and been rejected by Maffachufetts, Rhode Ifland, New Jerfey, and Maryland : it is now pending in New York, where it is faid it will alfo be rejected. I think I may fafely fay that this cry for paper money is not a popular cry; whilft thofe who afk it, refufe to give it currency, by refufing to part with their produce for it. Yet thefe fame patriots are conftantly reproaching the bank as the caufe of that want of credit, which themfelves occafion to the paper money.

The gentleman complained that the members of the committee of the late houfe were called upon to defend themfelves. It is true, they ftand charged with not having done their duty : but they are at liberty to defend themfelves againft the charge, if they can, or to let it alone. He faid alfo that it is indecent to inveftigate the proceedings of a former houfe of affembly. But if he examines the journals, he will find precedents ; and fee that other houfes have canvaffed the conduct of their predeceffors, and even that he has himfelf been an active agent therein. He muft not expect to efcape fcrutiny ; nor muft this houfe. Thofe amongft us, who may be returned to occupy thofe feats next year, may be called upon to juftify the conduct of this houfe, or of themfelves : for my part, I hope to retire, and remain a private citizen, which fuits both my inclination and affairs much better than to be in public life, for which I do not find myfelf very well qualified ; and am, therefore, inclined to leave my place to thofe that are. But fo long as I act a part in public life, fo long I expect my conduct to be examined : and however difagreeable this may be to fome gentlemen, there is no remedy but to bear it patiently.

All the gentlemen who have fpoken againft the bank, have plumed themfelves much upon a fuppofition that the learned counfel who pleaded the caufe of that inftitution before the late affembly, had conceded this point, that when the balance of trade is againft a country, a bank is injurious to that country. I am well acquainted with that gentleman's man's extensive abilities, and shall ever acknowledge them—but with all deference, I shall venture to say, that if he made such a concession, he was not authorised either by his employers, or by the fact. But was such a concession made? examine the whole of his reasoning on that point, he, I am authorised to say, considers it differently. Such a concession was neither intended nor meant to be made by him. The present state of our trade, when the balance is against us, may be, and is extremely injurious to the operations of the bank—not the bank injurious to trade or the country: and it is that which the learned counsel had in view, if I am not much mistaken.

The balance of trade is much spoken of in this debate: but I doubt if it be a subject well understood. Since the conclusion of the war, the balance of trade has been against us, and still continues to be so. The cause I have already stated in part, when I mentioned that the sanguine expectations which foreigners formed of reaping immense profits by adventuring to this country, had caused such vast importations of manufactures, as will require time to enable us to discharge the sum for which they were sold to our citizens.

The evils consequent to such immense importations, are at an end. The first adventurers have paid so dearly for their rash undertakings, and so many have been ruined, that this adventurous spirit is cured. Our own importers have been involved in the general calamity. Each imported goods agreeably to what he thought the wants of the country: and having sold them to shopkeepers and others, who, from the then state of cultivation of the country, and consequent deficiency of produce, were unable to pay, they are disabled from making remittances: and for want of those remittances, their credit, if not totally lost, is greatly injured in Europe; so that it will not speedily be in their power to renew excessive importations. This loss of credit may be considered in a two-fold point of view—either as a misfortune, or as of service to the country in general—which it will prove, is in the womb of time to shew: but I am of opinion, that wife laws, calculated to establish punctuality in our dealings, may turn the present loss of credit to future advantage. The people are falling into their former habits of industry and frugality. We may, therefore, reasonably expect that agriculture will flourish, and the state of cultivation in America surpass what was its most flourishing condition previous to the revolution. The balance of trade will then be

turned

turned in our favour: and specie will return as fast as it has lately been drained away. This situation of things is not very distant: and there is no occasion to destroy the bank on account of the balance of trade on which it has no influence.

It is said, that so great an estate as that of the bank, in the hands of a few, must be dangerous. This is supposing the capital of ten millions of dollars to be completed; and that in that case, it must carry all before it: whereas the present capital does not amount to one million, which belongs to many, and not to a few. And the stock cannot be accumulated, so as to be injurious, as the gentlemen assert, and still be confined to the hands of a few persons: for it can only accumulate by increasing the number of stockholders. I should not have touched upon this, but to shew the fallacy of their arguments.

The member from Cumberland complains, that the assembly which granted the charter, did not know the bye-laws and regulations previous to making the grant. True, they did not: and they must have been witches, indeed, to have known them, for I believe they were not then formed: but any thing will serve as a charge against the bank: and this may do as well as any of the rest.

He asks, "how can the farmers derive benefit from the "bank? If they cannot obtain loans, they cannot raise "produce; and they cannot have loans without a loan of-"fice; and without produce, we can have no trade; we "cannot have a loan office without paper money; and we "cannot get hard money to supply our necessities, for it is "in the bank," &c. &c. Having already answered in the course of the debate, those points which are urged and repeated again and again, without regard to what has been said in contradiction, or explanation—I shall now only observe, that so long as men are made as they are at present, they will cultivate the earth, and raise produce: whether this is effected by the mere efforts of industry, or with the aid of loans, is immaterial: and while there is produce to spare, there will be commerce. Therefore let the landed and commercial interest shake hands, for they do and must promote each others advantage.

This member again asserts, that there is not hard money sufficient for the establishment of a loan office—it is in the bank. A stranger hearing this complaint so often repeated, would suppose that all the hard money in the state was in the bank, and no possibility to come at it; that it was locked up there, and the people deprived of all use of it. Hundreds here present know the contrary. Whoever visits the bank, will see some people constantly bringing in money, and some taking it away:—the bank being, with respect to the circuletion of specie, as the heart to the circulation of blood.

The same gentleman says, that the bank has made sixteen per cent. by its stock, or perhaps more—and that this must be done by extortion. He should have been tender of making this charge without being possessed of proofs to support it. If he can prove it, I shall not offer another word in favour of the bank.

Mr. Whitehill. I did not say it was by extortion.

Mr. R. Morris. I shall not insist upon the matter, but shall take the gentleman's own explanation. I have already said, and I am warranted in asserting it, that the profits of the bank do not exceed 8 per cent. on an average. At the time the high dividends were made, the capital of the bank was small, and the exigencies of the united states required large advances and discounts—there were, besides, numerous private calls for discounts which could not be refused; and the directors were compelled to discount more heavily in proportion to their stock than they wished. During that period, the united states shared in those dividends of 10 to 16 per cent. per annum, and paid only 6 per cent. per annum for what they borrowed. These high profits arose from accidental circumstances, as I have mentioned, and, if needful, can prove—for I know the fact to be so.

In my notes I meet with a jumble of assertions made by this member—but no attempt to answer the arguments I offered yesterday. The gentleman asks, shall the state give way to the bank, or the bank to the state? and adds, that the bank should not interfere with the state. By the state I suppose he means a party in the state. I wish the state had not interfered with the bank—and the bank would never interfere with the state.

He speaks with severity of the trouble the house have had with the bank—how frequently it has been before the assemblies—and the waste of time and money thereby occasioned. The business of a bank was first brought before the assembly of this state, by recommendation of congress. It became a duty of the president and directors to apply to that house for a charter: they did so, and it was obtained. The second time the president and directors of the bank applied to the legislature, was in opposition to an application made by cer-

tain

tain perfons inimical to the exifting bank, for an act to eftablifh another. This attempt to eftablifh another bank, had for its object, the deftruction of the bank of North America. The motives were neither founded in reafon nor any defire to promote the public welfare: and the prefident and directors conceived it a duty due to their conftituents that they fhould come before that affembly and endeavour to fhew the pernicious tendency of that meafure. The third time they appeared, was in oppofition to certain petitions, praying to have their charter taken away. I fuppofe the gentleman thought them troublefome at that time, as well as now: but their appearance was then unavoidable. The petitioners in this third inftance, as well as in the fecond, brought them before the houfe. And how is the bank brought before us now, for the fourth time? The ftockholders had determined not to trouble us—they had determined on an appeal to another place: therefore the memorial of the prefident and directors prefented the laft feffion, is not the foundation of the prefent proceedings. But a large number of our fellow citizens have, by petition and memorial, called upon this houfe to repeal the law paffed laft year for annulling the charter of the bank. If the gentleman finds it troublefome to receive fuch petitions, let him fay fo; and not cry out againft the prefident and directors as if they caufed the trouble he complains of; for it is not fo.

The gentleman fays, this houfe does not know the ftate of the bank, or whether the prefident and directors are able to pay their notes. To which I anfwer, that this houfe has no right to know the ftate of the bank. We are not afked to truft them, or to take their notes. Thofe who entruft their money in the bank, or take its notes, may afk fuch queftions: but I believe they do not think it neceffary: if they did, I am perfuaded that full and ample fatisfaction would be given. He fays, that the memorialifts in favour of the bank, do not underftand the nature of it. I believe they know at leaft as much as the petitioners againft it. The memorialifts have pretty generally felt the benefits refulting from it:—thofe from the country, by finding a quick fale and ready money for their produce, and receiving this ready money at the bank, faw that the inftitution was beneficial and convenient: and fo feeing, they can eafily comprehend that the attempt to fupprefs it is injurious to the country.

As to the number of figners to thofe memorials or petitions in favor of the bank, this gentleman lays no ftrefs on
them:

them: for with proper exertions of induſtry, ſays he, twenty or thirty thouſand ſigners might be got to expunge the bank. In ſhort, this gentleman is conſtantly making aſſertions, which he cannot, or does not, ſupport with argument: and therefore I muſt meet him with an aſſertion in this point, which is, that with leſs exertion or induſtry can twenty or thirty thouſand ſigners be obtained in ſupport of the bank.

Having now done with the member from Cumberland, I proceed to examine the arguments adduced by a gentleman, * for whoſe underſtanding and abilities I have great reſpect; and who generally ſupports what he undertakes to defend, not only with ſtrength of reaſoning, but manages it with candour. I cannot, however, help obſerving, that he has deviated more from that candid line of conduct in this debate, than I have ever known him to do before.

He ſays the preſent houſe is not to enquire into what has been done by the late one—but whether ſufficient reaſons now exiſt, to warrant a renewal of the charter; and adds, that in all governments there muſt be a power lodged ſomewhere, which has a right to give and a right to take away.

I agree that in all governments, ſupreme power muſt be lodged ſomewhere. In ours, the aſſembly has the ſole right of granting charters—but no right to take them away. The power there goes on a different principle: and ſo it does in all except arbitrary governments. In Great Britain, the ſovereign grants charters, but he cannot take them away: the laws of the land have pointed out another mode of annulling them. As well may it be ſaid that the aſſembly of this ſtate, having exerciſed their ſovereign authority in the eſtabliſhment of a land office, from whence grants of lands are made to individuals, have a right to exerciſe the ſame ſovereign authority by deſtroying that office, and reſuming the lands again. This would be exerciſing the power to give, and the power to take away: but the aſſembly has no right to ſuch power: if it has, God help us! There are certain forms by which an individual may loſe his lands; but never, I hope, by a wanton act of legiſlative power. A conſiderable part of its time has been ſpent by this houſe in granting charters of incorporation to religious ſocieties, which are aſked for the purpoſe of enabling them to receive donations and legacies, for the ſupport of miniſters and payment of contingent charges, &c. If thoſe charters may be revoked at will, I ſhould not be ſurpriſed to ſee it done a few years hence, on ſome pretence or other.

* Mr. Finlay. What

What then is to become of the capital they may have respectively accumulated by means of the donations and legacies received in the mean time? Probably a certain gentleman, who is fond of escheats, may, if then in power, urge that the state should be heir to the corporations which suffer political death. What a hopeful situation must the country be in, under such systems as these! This gentleman says, let us examine our government—It is a democracy, and gives to all men equal rights: and agrarian laws may not be incompatible with the spirit of it: but we are not yet arrived at the period when such laws would be proper. I trust this member has better principles than to advocate so wicked a measure as a general division of property.

Mr. Finlay. I beg leave to explain. What I said, was, that agrarian laws would be unjust in our present situation.

Mr. R. Morris. They are unjust in all cases. The gentleman has remarked, "that wealth has a tendency to counteract our manners and the principles of our government. Why then should we give sanction, says he, to an institution founded on wealth? The stockholders must be men of wealth," &c.

If wealth be so obnoxious, I ask this gentleman why is he so eager in the pursuit of it? I frequently see him visiting the land office: Those visits, I presume, are not for pastime; although I do not doubt but they are for very proper purposes.——

Mr. Finlay. I never took up a foot of land in my life. What business I have transacted at that office, has been to serve others.

Mr. R. Morris. I have heard that some of the country gentlemen, whilst they are here attending in assembly, take up lands for their neighbours—and receive so much per cent. for transacting the business in the office.

Mr. Finlay. I must again set the gentleman right. I never received a farthing for such business in my life.

Mr. R. Morris. The gentleman has told us they had no banks in Rome, during the days of the republic. The Romans were a very different sort of people from the Pennsylvanians. They did in their days what they thought right and proper for them to do: but their conduct in this respect can never serve as a rule for ours.

"The object of the bank, he says, is gain—It is managed by themselves, that is, by the stockholders—and they have it always in view to *lift* their gain—Equality is the darling of our government—and the constitution says government is instituted to preserve equal privileges, &c.—the bank, he says, cannot be common amongst the citizens, and is therefore contrary to the constitution—and being perpetual, it is contrary to our laws, habits, manners," &c.

The charter of the bank being perpetual, is made use of as a strong argument against it: but really I do not know why we are told that the constitution is liable to change every seven years; and therefore it is inferred that the bank should not have longer duration: although the charter is perpetual, the stockholders are and will be constantly changing. It has been said that the charter is only a piece of paper, which the house may throw in the fire at pleasure. I say it did not derive its value from its being written on paper, but from having received the sanction of the legislature, which the house cannot so easily get rid of, as of the paper.

How does it appear that the bank is not common to our citizens? All of them who have money and inclination, may buy shares, or deposit there, at pleasure. How does it appear that the bank is contrary to our laws, habits, manners and customs? While the law incorporating the bank had existence, it certainly was consistent with our laws: and continues so now, while conducted as a private bank, against which there is no law. It consists well with our habits and customs—for we find the people in the daily habit and custom of lodging their money in the bank, and taking it away again at pleasure.

This gentleman has spoken of the low ebb of our commerce; and says it is almost entirely confined to importation: and he has remarked upon what fell from me, relative to Ireland not being a commercial nation. I hope I did not wound the gentleman's feelings, nor those of any other Irishman who heard me: it was far from my intention. I have been in Ireland—have experienced the hospitality of its inhabitants—and will venture to say, there are few people, not Irish, who entertain greater esteem for the country and people than I do: many of my intimacies are with gentlemen from that country—some of whom are now my hearers, and know the truth of what I say. All I meant was, that Ireland was not the most proper country in the world, to furnish us with precedents in commercial matters. I am not now to learn, that she exports large quantities of beef, butter and pork, and some manufactures: but still her trade is confined. I hope she has now laid the foundation for an

enlarged

enlarged commerce: and none will rejoice more than I shall, to see it extended to her greatest advantage.

The commerce of America is really, as the gentleman says, at a low ebb. It was on a much more respectable footing before the late war, than it is at present. We then exported large quantities of wheat, flour, Indian corn, beef, butter, pork, iron, lumber, and other articles, from this port. The neighbouring provinces made the like exports. New-England exported fish, oil, whalebone, &c. Maryland and Virginia, tobacco, provisions, iron, lumber, &c. North Carolina, naval stores; South Carolina and Georgia, rice, indigo, peltries, &c. and every part of the continent had staple commodities suited to the consumption of foreign markets, which enabled us to pay for the things we had occasion to import. Certain it is, that our exports are now much less than they were then, which is somewhat surprising, as every article of produce commands a good price, and nothing remains on hand to perish for want of purchasers. Whether this decrease of exports is the consequence of less culture of the country, or of an increased home consumption, I cannot decide. But this is certain, that the returning habits of industry, with the daily progress of population, must give an amazing increase of produce for exportation: and I should not be surprised, were this to happen much sooner than even the most sanguine expectations point out. If the position be true, that we are in a miserable situation so long as our imports exceed our exports—I hope it will be admitted, and soon be experienced, that the reverse of that position will place us in a flourishing state. But that the bank facilitates those importations, I have already denied; and have in some degree proved the contrary: and were it necessary, further proof might be adduced, although it seems improper to prove a negative.

The gentleman observes that after the establishment of the bank, a great number of bankruptcies happened. But what is this to the bank? If he means to charge the bank as the cause of them, he ought to have shewn it, and to have named the instances. But he could do neither the one nor the other. Those bankruptcies were occasioned by very different circumstances: particularly many of them were occasioned by the parties having at the approach of peace, (which they did not foresee or believe) imported or purchased large quantities of goods, which had cost the advanced prices of war time, with the high rates of freight and in-

surance

surance—so that from the large importations subsequent to the conclusion of peace, at a lower cost, and vastly cheaper rates of freight and insurance, they were disabled from selling those goods but at an immense loss. The vendues were crouded with them—those who were distressed, being forced to sell: and several who were able to stand the shock, have of those dear-bought goods, many on hands to this day. These are amongst the circumstances that brought on the greater part of those bankruptcies which are alluded to. But is the bank to be charged as accessory thereto, merely because they happened about that time? Surely not: on the contrary, many were saved by the seasonable aids which they derived from it.

He says the arts of the directors of the bank, to prevent exportation of specie, are contemptible. One of the charges made against the bank, is, that it has a direct tendency to banish specie: In defending it against this charge, it is first shewn that the bank is interested in preventing the export of specie; and then some of the means made use of, are mentioned: upon this, the cry is changed: the gentleman loses sight of the first charge, and exclaims that the arts used, are contemptible. Why should we not, says he, pay our debts, when we have contracted them? I agree that we ought and must pay our debts: and other means failing, the specie must go for the purpose: and as we agree in this, I hope he will also agree to exculpate the bank from the charge of banishing the specie: for the bank neither encourages, gives aid, or facility to the contracting of those debts: the bank gives neither credit nor security for debts contracted in Europe: and it is for the payment of those debts that specie is exported.

Our importations, he says, are too extensive. Agreed: but why bring this in as a charge against the bank? Has the bank engaged in commerce? Have the president and directors made any importations for the benefit of the institution? No. They are restrained by the charter from engaging in commerce.

The influence of the bank is again brought up. I have already observed, that such influence, if it exists at all, can never extend beyond the city: and even there, the necessity of sometimes refusing discounts, creates more enemies, than granting them makes friends. Probably, the gentleman may think that I stand indebted to this kind of influence for my seat in this house; but I promise him, that if I had thought

thought so, I would not have accepted it. I am of too independent a spirit to accept any station or office that can be offered to me, unless I were convinced that the offer was made from public confidence in my being able to render the service expected of me. This influence has never existed: neither my colleagues nor myself owe any thing to it.

The gentleman has found a very ingenious argument to prove that our present paper money has the confidence of the people—that is, its quick circulation. But I attribute that quickness of circulation to a totally different cause, viz. the want of that confidence. It began to be issued in July last: and nearly the whole of the emission had returned into the treasury in October or November. It was pushed from hand to hand, like the lighted stick in the play of " Jack's alive, and alive like, to be," each holder fearing that it should die in his hands ; and it is laughable to hear this gentleman congratulate the state on the returning confidence and virtue of the people, in receiving and paying this paper so quick. I must claim my share of this merit: for I acknowledge, I have assisted this quick circulation (so much admired by the worthy member) by parting with it as soon as possible after it came to my hands.

The memorial of the committee of merchants against paper money, is charged as proof against the bank on that subject : but even supposing the whole committee of merchants to be stockholders, the stock they may respectively possess, does not exceed two, three, four or five shares, amounting to 800, 1200, 1600, or 2000 dollars : and is this the great matter that could induce them to oppose paper money, if there were no other considerations? This interest in bank stock is not permanent—but changeable : and their shares, if they hold any, could only influence during the time they possessed them. But in common charity, these gentlemen ought to suppose that so respectable a set of men have some other principle of conduct than merely self-interest.

The letter from the president of the bank, offering a loan of money to the state, to prevent the necessity of issuing paper money, is now become a charge also, against the institution—because it is an evidence of the directors being opposed to paper money. Now, in my opinion, this letter proves their merit : they thought paper money would be injurious to the state ; and therefore they offered to lend what was wanted, rather than it should sustain that injury.

jury. It may be said they offered to lend what was wanted, rather than the bank should sustain the injury which paper money would do it. Agreed: the interest of the state and of the bank are the same in this, as they are in all other instances.

The opposers of the bank, we are told, have no private interest to serve by their opposition. But so long as they regard the bank and its supporters as one party, and themselves as another, they are as much interested in the question as their opponents. In fact, we have all one common interest in the welfare of our country: and although the defenders of the bank may have a small and separate interest in that institution, I am confident there is not one of us that would urge the restoring of the charter, if we regarded it as incompatible with the public welfare. The member from Westmoreland asks, can it be supposed that the gentlemen on his side of the question would oppose the bank from mere motives of envy? I believe that if they had been left fairly to themselves, they would not have opposed it at all—or at least that they would not now oppose it: but there are others at the bottom of this opposition—people who feel a political interest in the matter, whose suspicions have been roused, by the dread of phantoms presented to their imagination through the medium of envy and jealousy. I could speak plainer—but it is unnecessary.

This same gentleman draws a curious conclusion, from my having, as he states it, formed an expectation that the judges, however opposed individually to the bank, would in the courts decide in its favour. His conclusion is, that I depend on bank influence to obtain such a decision. But the question to be decided in the courts, is not whether the bank is useful or injurious? It is, whether a charter once granted, can be annulled without proof or even pretence of forfeiture? This is a general question, affecting all corporations: and however some of the judges might be inclined to oppose the bank, I still rest satisfied in my opinion of the integrity of their decision, and in my belief that they will be too regardful of their law characters, which become an object for history, ever to subject the judgment seat to reproach.

In reply to my observations respecting the difficulty of selling inward and purchasing outward cargoes for shipping, he asks, how were our ships loaded before the revolution? I answer, and the fact is well known, that delays frequently, I

may

may fay conftantly occurred for want of facilities in raifing money, and the merchant had it not always in his power to purchafe the produce brought to market by the farmer. The bank has remedied this inconvenience to both: deftroy the bank, and I have no doubt the cafe will again become familiar to the moft refpectable traders.

He has obferved that this is the only ftate *faddled* with a bank, altho' attempts to eftablifh them have not been wanting at Bofton, New York and Baltimore. But this obfervation will not ferve the gentleman. At Bofton they have an eftablifhed bank, countenanced and incorporated by the government. At New-York they have a bank; a charter has not been obtained—but I have been informed that it was withheld, when applied for, only becaufe the perfons applying for it, were obnoxious to government. The attempt to eftablifh a bank at Baltimore, failed for want of fubfcriptions to a fufficient amount of capital, and not for want of a charter. However, if the bank in this city be deftroyed, I venture to pronounce, that banks will foon be eftablifhed both in New-York and Baltimore: and our meafures will give great advantage to thofe places, which are ufually confidered as our dangerous rivals.

I might follow this gentleman's obfervations ftill further; but not having, on account of his abfence, been much ufed to his voice of late, and from his fpeaking rather low at times, I found difficulty in taking notes of all he faid. I wifh, however, that he had addreffed our underftanding, by fpeaking to facts—inftead of appealing to our feelings, by arguments drawn from what he calls the nature of things. In this he has fhewn more addrefs and judgment than candour.

Confidering what has fallen from the member from Montgomery county [mr. Lollar] this morning, as a kind of apology for what he faid on the firft day, I fhall pafs it over without remark, and proceed to make fome general obfervations.

The report of the committee of laft year contains matter of opinion only, and of opinions unfupported by fact. The bank is faid to be of no ufe to the farmer: I beg leave to afk, whether it is not ufeful to the farmer to meet a ready fale for his produce? If it be, I infift that the bank, in its operations, is ufeful to the farmer. I have heretofore experienced the inconvenience arifing from the want of a bank. When produce has been in plenty at market, and I been eagerly bent on the purchafe of it, although poffeffed of property

perty sufficient, I could not command money for the purpose; and the farmer could not sell upon credit: thus both have suffered distress, which would have been relieved by a bank. The exports in those days were very considerable:—the house of which I was then a member, have shipped in one year from forty to fifty thousand barrels of flour, and other articles in proportion. Such purchases required large sums of money: and these were extremely difficult to raise.

The quantity of produce for exportation, will now be increased every year: and the demand for money will also increase. If the bank be destroyed, the merchants of these days, will experience the difficulties I have mentioned. The farmers and millers bringing their produce to market, must wait for the sale, until money can be raised. They will be frequently compelled to sell at reduced prices, such as a chance monied man may please to offer: or they must place their goods in the hands of factors, who must derive their advantage by way of commission, storage, and charges, all which the farmer must pay. Whereas, if a bank is suffered to exist in full force, the merchant's occasional necessities can be relieved by discounts, and the farmer meet with ready sale for his produce. This I conceive to be the greatest use the farmers can wish to derive from the bank.

The first attack on the bank, gave a check to the price of produce, which has continued to be felt ever since: and if the bank be destroyed, those farmers who raise more than they consume, will become sensible of the consequences.

The bank, we are told, not only does not lend to the farmers—but prevents their getting money on loan. This I deny. Millers and farmers of responsibility, if they have connections in the city to indorse their notes, can procure discounts at the bank, as readily as the citizens of Philadelphia. In order to consider properly the charge that the bank prevents people from lending their money on bond and mortgage, which they say it effects, by the enormous dividends drawn upon bank stock, it is necessary to state the amount of that stock, and to whom it belongs:——

The stock at present amounts to 870,400 dollars, which, divided by 400, gives 2176 shares, whereof 285 shares belong to foreigners, of which nine tenths to Holland. None of the money invested in these shares, would, if there was no bank, be lent in this state upon bond and mortgage, we may safely conclude. Various have been the applications made by our citizens to borrow money in Europe, particularly

larly in Holland: and altho' the beſt landed ſecurity which this country affords, has been offered, yet every application has failed; and not a ſingle ſhilling has been obtained that I could ever learn. Six hundred and ſix ſhares belong to inhabitants of New Hampſhire, Maſſachuſetts, Connecticut, New York, New Jerſey, Delaware, and Virginia: a conſiderable part of theſe ſhares were ſubſcribed during the war, by perſons ſtimulated thereto by the belief that placing a part of their funds in the bank of North America, would afford a great aid to the cauſe of the united ſtates. Theſe ſhares are divided among many individuals: can it, therefore, be believed, that any part of the money paid for theſe ſhares, would, upon a diſſolution of the bank, be lent upon bond and mortgage to our citizens? If thoſe ſtockholders were diſpoſed to lend in that manner, it would, doubtleſs, be in their own reſpective ſtates, to their own fellow-citizens, within their own view, and within the protection of thoſe laws under which they live.—Six ſhares are held by inhabitants of Cheſter county, one by an inhabitant of Lancaſter, five by inhabitants of Weſtmoreland, twelve by inhabitants of Berks, twelve by inhabitants of Bucks, and fourteen by inhabitants of Philadelphia county. Theſe fifty ſhares were probably ſubſcribed on the ſame patriotic principles: and, if the bank were deſtroyed, it is poſſible that this money, or ſome part of it, might be lent upon bond and mortgage. But the whole amount of fifty ſhares is only 20,000 dollars: and it is doubtful whether any part of even this pittance would be ſo lent out. The remaining ſhares, being 1235, belong to citizens of Philadelphia, and principally to the commercial men, whoſe greateſt inducement to continue ſtockholders, is to ſupport an inſtitution which affords them accommodation and convenience, by means of diſcounts. With a very few exceptions, we may ſay that not one dollar of this money, would ever be lent out on bond and mortgage. There are very few if any of this claſs of ſtockholders who do not ſtand in need of the whole of their money in the courſe of buſineſs; and when in need, they borrow occaſionally perhaps the whole amount, or more: It is upon theſe principles, the merchants generally remain ſtockholders—when one does not want his money, it is earning his ſhare of the dividend from another: and by thus clubbing a capital together, as it were, the occaſional wants of all are ſupplied. But I am perfectly ſatisfied,

that

that none of the money paid for thefe fhares, can be lent on bond and mortgage. Does it not, therefore, appear that this charge is as groundlefs as the others?

Before the war, monied men were fond of lending upon bond and mortgage: it was a favourite practice; was thought perfectly fafe; and enabled thofe who were advanced in years, to receive an income, fo as to live at eafe and quiet; and I doubt not this practice might have been revived, had not moft of thofe lenders fuffered feverely—fome in the whole —and others in part; and even thofe who have efcaped lofs, are deterred from lending again by the dread of paper money and tender laws; and fo long as this dread continues, all hopes muft be relinquifhed, of borrowing upon bond and mortgage.

Whilft the practice of lending upon bond and mortgage exifted, there was another practice exifted with it. The lenders were chiefly citizens; and for the convenience of collecting the intereft on the day it fell due, they preferred lending to thofe citizens of Philadelphia, who wanted to borrow; fo that the farmers, even in thofe days, could not obtain loans, until the citizens were fatisfied; now, fhould the days of loaning return, the bank will prove ufeful to the country in that refpect; for by the temporary difcounts which citizens obtain at the bank, it is probable that moft of their wants may be fupplied, and thereby their competitions with the farmers be prevented. I have known many a man formerly obliged to borrow money for twelve months, although he only wanted it for three, four or fix; but the practice was to lend for twelve; and the capitalifts thought it too troublefome to lend for a fhorter time. A certain rich citizen of Philadelphia, inimical to the bank, now taken and hugged to the bofoms of thofe gentlemen who fo warmly advocate the intereft of the farmers, declares publicly, that he is an enemy to the inftitution becaufe he could purchafe flour cheaper, were it deftroyed. From this declaration, the farmers may form fome judgment how far the bank is ufelefs or injurious to them.

In effect, the utility of the bank is experienced by every man in the ftate, at fome period or other. I have fhewn clearly it is ufeful to the farmer and miller. The mechanic derives alfo his fhare of benefit and convenience from this inftitution. Punctuality in paying his workmen is of great advantage to the mafter, and abfolutely neceffary to the comfortable fubfiftence of the journeymen. The employer muft

have

have it in his power to make regular payments to the master mechanic,—or he, in his turn, cannot be punctual. It has heretofore happened, that those who built houses, or gave employment to various trades, have not had it in their power to pay punctually, according to their engagements. The like may be expected again. But in all such cases, on future occasions, relief may be found at the bank. The employer, giving his note to the master, their joint credit, if they are entitled to credit, will procure the sum wanted, by discount at the bank. This observation must strike every mechanic at the first glance; and, if he turns his attention to the subject, his own thoughts will point out various modes by which he may draw resources and conveniences from this institution. In short, the same reasoning will apply to every description of men that have any thing to do with money.

Is it possible, then, that we shall pursue measures for the destruction of an institution so useful? One would think that the first thing which offers itself to our consideration, on the nature of a bank, would be sufficient to prevent the pursuit of such a measure. It is, that a number of persons have placed in the care of the president and directors of the bank a sum of money for the express purpose of lending to those that want to borrow; and this sum those persons (stockholders) cannot draw out again; but it must remain for that use. Besides this, there is also a further sum constantly in the power of the directors, which enables them to extend their loans beyond the capital or stock; and on which part of the profits of the bank arise. The integrity, punctuality and prudence of the president and directors have obtained such credit with the citizens of Philadelphia, that numbers of them deposit their money in bank for safety and convenience. It is received and paid at their pleasure, without expence or risque to the depositor. And the sums so collected to a point, being considerable, the bank is enabled always to lend a part of the money so placed: as it is not in the nature of things that the depositors should all call for their money at one and the same time—consequently, a part of the sum will answer the demands of the whole; and by this means, it must be seen, that sums of money are constantly brought into circulation and use, that would otherwise lie mouldering in the chests of those who would neither lend nor use them; and that the bank, by this credit, is enabled to extend its utility amongst those whose necessities,

H disappointments,

disappointments, interest, or convenience, incline them to borrow.

I have been frequently told, out of doors, although it has not been mentioned here—indeed it could not with propriety be mentioned here—that the opposition to the bank is in part levelled at me personally. If any oppose it in that view, and suppose that my interest would suffer by the annihilation of the bank, they are grosly mistaken. I am not stimulated by the consideration of private interest, to stand forth in defence of the bank: for be assured, sir, that if this be destroyed, another shall arise out of its ashes—one that will be of great advantage to my interest, and to the interest of those who may join me in the establishing it: nay, should I be disappointed in procuring such associates as I would choose in the undertaking, I will establish a bank on my own capital, credit, and resources; and so far from doubting its success, I do not hesitate to pronounce that even my enemies (and God knows I seem to have enough of them—at least political enemies—for I know of no other cause for their being so)—will deal with and trust me; not that I expect they may like me better then than now; but they have confidence in me; and, for the sake of their own interest and convenience, they will deal with me.

The gentleman from Westmoreland has acknowledged the utility of the bank during the war; and has drawn a comparison between it and the continental army. The continental army, says he, were useful during the war: and yet we disbanded them. But surely they were not disbanded because they had been useful—but because, when peace was established, they were no longer necessary. He acknowledges that this institution was useful; and yet endeavours to abolish it—because it has been said that it was injurious.

He also made a comparison between the bank and general Washington. I have ever acknowledged the services and merits of that great man. His utility during the war will never be denied: and in his resignation, he acted consistently with that noble and disinterested spirit by which he had been actuated during his command. He did what was expected of him: and it will ever be a part of my pride to join in paying him every tribute of praise. But this comparison ought not to have been made; the general's acceptance of command, and the establishment of the bank, are very different things; and took place on very different principles. The first was the patriotic act of a noble mind, which had not only the
service

service of his country, but also honour and glory in view. The last arose from necessity, having also the service of the country for one part of its object; and the interest and emolument of those who should engage in it, for the other: The country has received the service: and now endeavours are used to requite it with ingratitude. But further services and benefits may be expected by America from this bank. We are now at war with the Algerines. Every one knows that peace must be purchased of them with arms or with money. In either case, money is necessary: and we know that the most pressing requisitions of congress, do not prevail with the states to raise it as fast as they ought: nay, whilst the several states are deliberating whether or how they shall raise money, one part of the citizens of the united states are plundered of their property by the seizure of their ships and cargoes; and another part of them are condemned to slavery. Let us suppose that the commissioners employed for the purpose, had so far succeeded, that the Algerines had agreed to make peace, on the receipt of a sum of money—where shall congress get the money? We have not so well enabled them to acquit their engagements in Europe, as to afford any reasonable prospect that they can borrow more: But upon such an occasion, this institution—the bank—might again be of essential service to the united states. In this state, we are now threatened with internal troubles at Wioming: no person can tell what may happen in that quarter: if things go on as they have done, we may be in want of every aid. Where are we to find sudden resources, or the sums that may become necessary to put an end to those troubles, and extend the protection of government over the boundaries of the state? Various circumstances tend to shew, that upon this and every proper occasion, the government of Pennsylvania might be sure to command every aid and assistance which the bank can give: And shall we then, from a mere pretended opinion that this institution has been injurious, " rip up the goose that lays the golden eggs?"

Mr. Smilie said the gentleman had assumed another ground. The debate had, until that stage, been conducted with decency—how far he [mr. Morris] had departed therefrom, he left those present to judge. The members opposed to the bank were by him charged directly with speculating in the depreciation of the paper money—and indirectly with perjury. He might be under the necessity of recriminating. If he should be obliged to touch upon any circumstances of that gentleman's gentleman's private conduct, he hoped he would bear it patiently.

Ordered, that the further confideration of the report be poftponed.

Adjourned.

Saturday, April 1, 1786, A. M.

RESUMED the confideration of the report of the committee, to whom were referred the memorials praying a repeal or fufpenfion of the law annulling the charter of the bank.

Mr. Fitzfimons. After the able difcuffion which this fubject has undergone, little feems to be left for me to fay. My worthy colleague, whofe knowledge and experience are fo fuperior to mine, has gone largely into it : but as appeals have been made by our opponents to the feelings of the farmer and the tradefman—and as he has left fome points untouched—I muft pray the attention of the houfe, while I endeavour to make fome obfervations on them.

If there appears to have been any attempt at reafoning, by thofe who are oppofed to the refolution, it has been by the member from Weftmoreland. That gentleman has the capacity of ftating clearly, and reafoning juftly. If he has failed in either, on the prefent occafion, it muft be imputed rather to the badnefs of the caufe he has undertaken, than to the want of ability in himfelf.

To his reflections upon government, I fhall make little reply. If our habits and our circumftances are not well adapted to our frame of government, it is the fault of thofe who made it : for our habits and our circumftances were nearly the fame as they are at prefent, when the conftitution was formed.

His obfervations upon trade, being drawn from theory, it would be improper to remark feverely on them : but it may not be unufeful to fhew they are not well grounded.

His arguments went to prove, that our imports exceeding our exports to a very great amount, muft prove injurious— in fhort, they went to prove, that our trade, as it is at prefent, ought not to be encouraged. But thefe opinions, as well as fome others that have been advanced in the courfe of this debate, have been taken upon truft : and though they may correfpond very well with the fituation of Weftmoreland county, and fome others which are not within reach of

a feaport

a seaport to dispose of their products—it will be difficult to persuade those farmers who have been accustomed to bring the produce of their industry to this city, and receive money for it, that trade is injurious. I believe experience has fully proved the contrary; and that the commerce of Pennsylvania has been eminently useful in promoting and encouraging its agriculture and improvements.

As to the trade of import, which the gentleman conceives to operate so forcibly to our ruin, I do not wonder he should not be well informed respecting it: as I find many hold that opinion, who have better means of information. Immediately after the peace took place, the importations were very great. The people in Europe seem to have considered Philadelphia as the emporium of America; and directed their operations to it accordingly: but does that gentleman know what part of those importations was again exported? Does he know that we have usually imported for the consumption of West Jersey, Delaware, the Eastern Shore of Maryland—and that almost every state in the union derived supplies of European goods from us—after those great importations were made—and that this state derived a very considerable revenue upon their consumption? An impost of 100,000l. per annum, paid into the treasury, ought to convince the gentleman, that trade even to him is not unuseful—he has a share of that revenue.

Amsterdam imports from all parts of the globe, and to an immense amount. Are the United Netherlands, or the province of Holland, ruined by those importations?—or are they not rather the source of their wealth? That city pays two-fifths of all the expences of the states: Philadelphia has paid in nearly the same proportion, of all the expences of Pennsylvania. Philadelphia was likely to become the Amsterdam of America: but the gentlemen from Fayette, Westmoreland, &c. being such adepts in the science of commerce, have taken effectual measures to prevent it.

In the gentleman's observations upon commerce, he had almost forgotten our exports—" a little flaxseed,"—but not worth mentioning.

There have been shipped from this port 14,000 hogsheads of tobacco, in a year, at 3l. per hhd. worth 42,000l. exclusive of freight; 40,000 barrels of flour; 300,000 bushels of wheat; with a variety of other articles: which are surely of some value.

We were not only the importers for other states, but the

exporters likewife. In the year 1784, 12,000 hogfheads tobacco, the produce of Virginia and Maryland, were fhipped from this port. It appears by the returns from the cuftomhoufe, that 1116 fail of veffels entered and cleared at it laft year: the value of the cargoes of fuch a number, muft furely be of fome confequence. But whatever may have been the advantages of this commerce, I repeat it—our own unwife reftrictions will operate to leffen them.

That the extent of our importations has been injurious to the ftate, is become a fafhionable doctrine: it is propagated to ferve fome purpofe, and has obtained credit: but how does this appear? The value of our imports may be pretty accurately known, by the books of the collector: but the proportion of them fold to the ftates around us, which go by land, or by inland navigation, cannot be afcertained. The exportation of fpecie is the proof principally relied on, and from thence the ruin of the ftate is predicted. For my own part, I fee money exported with as little reluctance as I fee any other merchandize—I confider it but as a merchandize, —and that if we export it at one time, we fhall import it at another. I wonder how we obtained this money—Pennfylvania has neither gold or filver mines—but fhe has what is better, and what will purchafe gold and filver at all times. This complaint, however, of the export of fpecie, does not come well from the advocates of paper money. I think a very common affertion of theirs, is—that a virtuous people can live without gold or filver: and they would all wifh to be thought virtuous.

It appears to me a little paradoxical, that an importation of an over proportion of goods can be injurious to a country. It does not follow, that becaufe the merchants import more goods than are neceffary, that the people fhould buy more than they want. It may poffibly oblige the importer (as has been the cafe in many inftances) to fell them for lefs than coft: but furely the lofs there muft be to the feller, and not to the buyer: and as the fellers on thofe terms, have been generally foreigners, the lofs has been theirs, and the gain been ours. It may have been a temptation to unthinking people to buy more than they had occafion for—and our merchants have fuffered in the fale of fuch goods as they had on hand, which muft have been caufed by the low price of the others: but it is a novel complaint, that a choice of goods, to be bought at lefs than their coft, fhould be an injury to the purchafer.

To

To complain of the want of money, is not peculiar to the prefent times. Such complaints always have, and always will be made. I think the average price of flour, during the laft year, would be near 50s. for the barrel (1cwt. 3qrs.); of wheat, 9s. per bufhel; of flaxfeed, 15s. per bufhel; and immediate fale, and payment on delivery. This, furely, did not argue a want of money. Was there any part of the produce of the country brought to market, that could not be fold for ready money, and at a very high price? I believe not.

I am ready, however, to acknowledge that this is not the cafe at prefent. The produce of the country has fallen in price: and, what is worfe, there are not purchafers for it, at any price. If I were to affert that this is owing in part to a ftoppage of difcount at the bank, perhaps it would be controverted—I leave thofe that would controvert it, to account for it otherwife.

Thus much I have thought neceffary to fay upon the fubject of commerce, that the pofitions laid down by the gentleman from Weftmoreland, might not be taken for granted.

As he was obliged to acknowledge that the bank was ufeful to commerce, he meant to fhew that commerce was injurious to the ftate; and of courfe, that the bank, which gave facility to that commerce, was neceffarily injurious.

Upon the fubject of the bank, I have yet faid very little: my worthy colleague has explained its ufefulnefs very fully. From the arguments ufed againft it, we would be led to infer, that the money locked up in its vaults, is ufelefs to the good people of the ftate; and that if it were not for fuch an inftitution, the whole of that money would be lent out on bond or mortgage in the country. Let us examine if this is really the cafe.

If this money was not in the bank, would it neceffarily be lent out in the country? Or, being in the bank, is it therefore unemployed? It is eafy to prove that neither of thefe is the cafe.

Of the prefent ftock of the bank, 360,000 dollars are the property of perfons who are not inhabitants of, or refident in Pennfylvania: and I believe it will not be pretended that the owners of that part of the ftock would fend it to Pennfylvania, to be lent out at intereft. There is yet no inftance of foreigners lending money in this ftate on private fecurity. And fuch of the ftockholders as are citizens of the fifter ftates, would not be likely to fend it here for that purpofe— becaufe the rate of intereft is as high, at leaft, in the other

ftates

ſtates as in Pennſylvania—and there is as good ſecurity there. Of the remaining ſtock, near 500,000 dollars are the property of people in and near the city, divided among about two hundred and fifty perſons: moſt of thoſe are in buſineſs, and became ſtockholders to encourage the inſtitution, becauſe it operates to their convenience, and becauſe they can borrow not only as much as they own of the ſtock, but much more, according to their credit and circumſtances.— Very few of them, however, could put their money out to intereſt. Few of the merchants of the preſent day, have money beyond their immediate occaſions: if this is the caſe— and I believe it cannot be diſproved—very little, if any of the preſent capital would be lent out in the country at intereſt, though there had never been a bank.

But does it follow that the money's being in the bank renders it leſs uſeful to the citizens? Surely it does not. The dividends made to the ſtockholders prove that it is all employed: and whatever the dividend exceeds the common intereſt of money, proves that more is circulated than its ſtock: of courſe, ſo much is added to the circulation beyond the actual ſpecie.

There can be no method by which the circulation is better aſſiſted than by a bank of depoſit and diſcount, ſuch as the bank of North America is. Among trading people, where there are no banks, every merchant or trader muſt at all times have money in his cheſt or in his drawer unemployed: if a man is in the receipt of money, he cannot lay it out again the day he receives it. If he wants to make a purchaſe of any conſiderable value, he collects money for ſome time in order to enable him to make that purchaſe; or, if he has bought on credit, he collects to make good his payment when it becomes due: by this means it muſt happen, that a conſiderable part of the money uſed in that place, muſt every day be abſolutely uſeleſs. But where there is a bank, a trader, when he receives money, ſends it there, for theſe reaſons—that it is kept in ſafety, without any expence; that the more he keeps there, the better credit he has; and that if he occaſionally borrows, his making depoſits of money is an inducement to the directors to lend to him. By keeping the money there, the whole ſum, which would have lain in the hands of the different owners, is collected together; and as all the owners never want their money on the ſame day, the bank is enabled to lend for ſhort periods a certain part of that money; and thereby give that part circulation, which would

would otherwife be ufelefs. Thus it appears that collecting money in a bank, increafes the circulation: and the utmoft that the country gentlemen can any ways contend for, is—that they, living at a diftance, and wifhing to be accommodated with loans of money for long periods, cannot have them at the bank. But is that a reafon that the inhabitants of the city and its vicinity fhall not have the privilege of accommodating each other? Though the money is not lent to the farmer, yet, as it facilitates the purchafe of his products, and the procuring him ready money for them, he derives thereby a full fhare of the advantage.

Another objection has been artfully made to the operations of the bank, which deferves notice: viz. that the aid it gives the merchant, enables him to keep up his goods till he can obtain a better price for them, than if they were to be immediately fold. This objection is more plaufible than folid. It is in the nature of trade, that when it is free, the profit is foon reduced as low as the trade will admit: it muft afford fufficient for the encouragement of thofe concerned in it, or they will leave it off: if it exceeds that proportion, for any time, fo many will engage in it, as to reduce the profit.

If, when a fhip arrives, the merchant can, by a loan of money from the bank, difpatch her again immediately, fhe performs, perhaps, two voyages more in the year, than if he is obliged to detain her till the cargo is fold: and this will certainly enable him to fell his goods cheaper, or to give more for the products of the country. A moderate capital, fuch as ours generally are, turned four times a year, will enable the merchant to fell for a lefs profit than if he turns it but twice. So that in every view in which this inftitution is taken, it will be found advantageous.

With refpect to the liberality of its management, the inftances are innumerable. When the legiflature of this ftate were unable to pay the officers of their army, they granted them certificates; and mortgaged the revenue of the excife for payment of the intereft. When the intereft became due, the revenue was not collected; and the diftrefs of the officers was great. On that occafion, without any particular application, the bank advanced the money; and took the reimburfement when the revenue was collected.

At the time when its aid to the united ftates had put it out of the directors' power to make private difcounts, they, upon on an application of the legiflature, advanced 5000l. for the defence of the frontiers.

I remember when the enemy's row boats took veffels within our port, and carried them off: and the ftate had not the means of granting protection againft fo inconfiderable, tho' infulting an enemy. On that occafion, the bank, by an advance of about 25,000l. enabled the merchants to fit out a fhip, which, within a few days, not only cleared the bay and river, but captured a cruizer of twenty guns, belonging to the Britifh fleet.

The inftances of its fervices are innumerable. Afk the managers of the houfe of employment: they will tell you the poor could not be fed without the affiftance of the bank. —Afk the wardens of the city; and they will tell you that the city could not now be lighted but by means of the loans obtained there. But it is needlefs to repeat the inftances: for I may fay there is no fervice, public or charitable, to which its affiftance has been denied. Perhaps its ufe will be better underftood when the want of it is fufficiently felt—and though the prefent attempt to crufh it may fucceed for a time, I have no doubt it will be as eagerly called for as it is now decried.

I cannot help obferving, that there are gentlemen in this houfe, who fometimes inftruct—but oftener infult us with their reading—One has brought us an extract from the journals of the Irifh commons, to prove that the people of Ireland were oppofed to the eftablifhment of a bank. Several writers have treated on the fubject of banking—one, a writer in great repute, Mr. Smith, who treated on the wealth of nations, ftates that the trade of Glafgow was doubled in 15 years after the eftablifhment of a bank there—and that improvements of every kind kept pace with that increafe. Thus if banks were regarded as injurious in fome places, they have been found beneficial in others.

Mr. Smilie. This fubject has been fo ably handled by the gentlemen who have fpoken againft the report under the confideration of the houfe, that it is not requifite to enter deeply into it. It is however neceffary to take notice of fome remarks which have fallen from the gentlemen in favour of the report.

Great ftrefs is laid on one circumftance, and a loud clamour raifed, becaufe the committee of laft year did not go to the bank. But I would afk, what enquiry fhould we have made at the bank? What information would have been afforded

forded us there? Would the directors have laid open their books to us? I remember well a question put to the directors by the committee who made the report before us, were they willing to give information to the committee consistent with the secrecy of the institution? If the committee of last year had called, they would not have laid open their books. And if the committee had enquired how far the president and directors had abused the trust reposed in them, it would have been altogether useless and unnecessary. This being the case, the committee were perfectly right in not calling at a place where they could not obtain the intelligence requisite. There was another reason: the bank not being under the control of government, the committee could not oblige them to lay before them a state of their accounts, or their books.

Some of the arguments on this question have been so much refined as to be above the comprehension of us country people. A gentleman tells us, that the balance of trade is a mere speculation. I must confess I am not much acquainted with trade—but I know there is some such thing as a balance of trade—and that it is greatly against this country at present.

The question of right in this house to take away a charter, has been pretty well discussed, and it now seems well understood. Two of the members on the other side have conceded the point. The others have not—but their arguments amount to that, when our situation is considered. As charters are granted by the assembly—they can be revoked no other way than by the assembly. They cannot be taken away by the courts of justice, as they are given by the legislature.

It has been said, that the bank is dangerous to the state, and in support of this, the plan of mortgaging to it the revenues has been adduced. The gentleman who proposed this plan, replies, that he was not authorised by the directors to make the proposal to this house. Another member who is one of the bank directors, tells us the same thing. But really I can hardly stretch my credulity so far, as to believe that to be the case. If it was, I do not scruple to say, it was an insult to this house, to propose to them the adoption of a measure, to which if they had acceded, they would have left it in the power of the directors to laugh at them.

The gentlemen in favour of the present report, have manifested

nifested a violent degree of resentment against the committee of last year, who made the report relative to the bank—at the same time they seem desirous to keep clear of the late house. But if the committee were wicked, the house must have been no less criminal—as they must have been either ignorant, or equally wicked. The policy of this proceeding, is easily seen. There were no hopes of changing the minds of the members of the committee of last year, now in this house—therefore it was not judged necessary to keep any measures with them—but the late house is treated with more lenity, in hopes that some of its members now here, might come over in favour of the bank. One gentleman [mr. Fitzsimons] wishes he could separate the committee from the house, and make them personally responsible. Had he proposed to impeach them, he would have shewn a more manly spirit, and not a worse disposition. But the committee as well as the house of last year, are accountable only to their country, which will judge of their conduct.

A gentleman from the city, [mr. Morris] has called upon us to shew abuses in the conduct of the directors of the bank. I am in possession of one fact—which, however, I shall not mention, unless I am urged to it.—

The same gentleman has asserted, that the public creditors would have been better paid, had the paper not been struck—if the impost duties had been collected. That they were not collected, was not the fault of the late house—it arose from the misconduct of some of the officers whose duty it was to collect them. But the last house could not pay the public creditors without the paper money.

The gentleman mentions the endeavours of the directors of the bank to prevent usury. But here facts stand in our way. Can any gentleman say that usury was not coeval with the bank? The five per cent. per month is too well known, and its effects too sensibly felt, to render it necessary to do more than barely mention it. All this was unknown before the establishment of the bank.

He seems to call in question the understanding of the late committee and asks, were they able or willing to consider the subject of the bank in every point of view? As to capability, I am not disposed to contend with him on that head—I shall readily admit him my superior. The gentleman then gives us a high encomium on the services of the bank during the late contest—and tells us of his having lodged 4 or 5000 barrels of flour in the camp of general Washington,

ington, on his own account. But it is not to him nor to the bank we are indebted for our independence—I should be glad it was ascertained to whom we owe that event—there are so many claimants, that it should be decided on. A certain writer, a friend of that gentleman's, lays claim to a great share of it—I wish they would settle it between them.

The gentlemen in favour of the report have laboured hard to shew the dreadful consequences of meddling with property. But what right of property has been invaded by the repealing act? If it had, indeed, confiscated the property of the stockholders, and applied it to the use of the state, then there might be some foundation for such an argument. No such thing has been done or even attempted. The assembly only determined that the bank should not be held under their charter. Will any man say that property may not be applied to improper uses? Suppose a man had a mind to employ his property in erecting magazines and laying by military stores, has not the assembly a right to pass a law to prevent him?

The gentleman is exceedingly hurt at the repetition of paper money—in our speeches. But the bank is as dear to him as the paper money is to us, and as frequently occurs in his speeches. I have lately read a pamphlet on paper money—and all the writer says on the subject, is, what an old German told him a long time ago—viz. That paper was paper—and money was money. But if an unprincipled author, who lets out his pen for hire, had so far relaxed in his last performance that his employers would not pay him for it—if he, in want of his food, in passing through the market, should find a five shilling bill in his pocket, and, going to a tavern, procure for it his dinner, and a pot of beer, he would be apt then to cry out—This paper money, I find, after all, is victuals and drink to me.

The directors of the bank are chosen by the stockholders, who vote in proportion to their property. If we examine this mode, we shall find it highly dangerous: as all is done by nine or ten men—so that the bank will remain under the present directors, during their lives, which is a direct tyranny, they being the representatives of a few men only.

A gentleman from the city [mr. R. Morris] thanked God that the bank is not under the control of government. At a former day he was of a different opinion—[Here mr. Smilie read two articles of the proposals for forming the bank—signed by Mr. Morris—wherein the clause subjecting the accounts

accounts of the bank to the inspection of the superintendent of finance, is praised and styled excellent.]

It appears by these articles that he thought it an excellent part of the plan of the bank that it should be under the control not only of congress, but of the state—but it must be considered that he, as superintendent of finance, was the person who had the control of it. So that at different times, he entertains different sentiments on the subject.

The gentleman tells us the state has not credit—that it is too powerful to have it. But if the state has not credit, how can it communicate credit to the bank? And if the bank has credit, why ask it of this house?

I now refer to one of the notes I took while this gentleman was speaking yesterday. He tells us that the members in favour of paper money, seek it, for the purpose of paying off debts at an under value——

Mr. R. Morris. I did not make the charge the gentleman says, only against the members in favour of paper money, but I meant to include the advocates of it in general. I desire that my words may be taken in their true sense. This charge has not originated with me—It has been made from one end of the continent to the other—in news papers, in public debates—and in private conversation—so that it is no new thing.

Mr. Smilie on this declared himself satisfied with the explanation given by mr. Morris—and said he should not pursue the course he had proposed to himself in his discourse.

Mr. Morris declared it was not his wish or desire to prevent the member from taking the fullest latitude. He had a fair opportunity. Mr. Morris added he had not risen with a view to hinder it.

Mr. Smilie. The gentleman made some observations on the members from the country speculating in lands and receiving so much per cent. for what business they transact——

Mr. Morris said a note had just been put into his hand, stating that a member then in the house would, if called upon, prove what he said relative to some of the members receiving so much per cent for transacting their neighbours business.

Mr. Smilie. What other members may do, I know not—but I have transacted a great deal of business for my neighbours, and have never received a copper for it. I do not know that it would be criminal to receive payment—nor do

I know

I know who the gentleman means to charge. This information I regard as addressed to the galleries.

It is denied that the bank facilitates commerce. But I think it is evident that it does. Cargoes of goods have been purchased in one day, which could not have been the case but for the bank. The bank, making it convenient to get money, facilitates the purchase of goods. It will not be controverted that goods are purchased quicker by its means, than they possibly could without it.

We are told that the friends of the bank have given support and countenance to the paper money. I do not pretend to assert the contrary. But I have heard it strongly asserted. A gentleman says that a discount on the paper money of from $2\frac{1}{2}$ to 5 per cent may be had. If such depreciation has taken place, it is occasioned by the bank; as it does not receive the paper money: and consequently persons indebted to that institution are obliged to procure hard money at all events—so that the bank is the cause of discount being given.

The same gentleman seems to consider us as mere machines. He says, if we were left to ourselves, we would not be now opposed to the bank. I have never been urged to my opposition—I have opposed the bank from conviction that the charter was incompatible with the welfare of the state—and I concluded it must be destroyed. What! does he suppose we are duped, or that we are dishonest? If we were capable of being bought off, it must be acknowledged we have not among us persons capable to purchase. If any members of this house were corrupt enough to betray for reward the trust reposed in them, the gentlemen on the other side have the means in their hands to prevail on them.

Mr. R. Morris. I said that a person possessed of considerable wealth, opposed to the bank from private views, was hugged in the bosoms of those inimical to that institution from other considerations, although there is no other tie or connection between them.

Mr. Smilie. I have never been attempted by any such person. I have taken up the matter upon higher ground: and as to what the gentleman who spoke yesterday in favour of the bank, said, respecting the attack upon that institution being levelled at him personally, I must declare that I have been been actuated by no such motive. As a private citizen, I respect him—although as a politician, I happen to differ from him in sentiment.

To conclude: We have now no bank. The question, therefore,

therefore, is, whether we shall have a bank or no?—not barely whether we shall have a bank—but whether we shall have such a bank as we had before? for no modification is offered—the report before the house proposes to revive the old charter. Are we prepared to agree to such a report? Are we prepared to give a charter empowering the corporation of the bank to hold ten millions of dollars—and that in what kind of property they please? When I look round me, and see so many independent members, I feel a confidence that they will never agree to vest the powers consequent to such a property in a board of directors chosen by six or seven stockholders. Fears and jealousies were entertained at the time of granting the charter, when the doctrine of banking was but little understood : and two attempts were made to limit it : they then only looked forward to the ill consequences to be apprehended from it. We have seen some of them : I therefore trust, that instead of restoring the charter, in order, as the report says, to restore the honour of the state, we shall save it from that instrument of destruction.

Dr. Logan declared he esteemed himself so unqualified for a discussion of the question under debate, that he had not proposed to trouble the house, by rising to speak to it. Being entirely disinterested in the matter, he had resolved to give his vote according as he should be convinced ; and was sorry to see that the gentlemen opposed to the bank, instead of answering the arguments made use of on the other side, had recourse to personalities. The bank, at its first establishment, had been conducted on such narrow principles, as to induce numbers of gentlemen to unite in their endeavours to establish another, which had induced the president and directors to alter their plan. He had then become a subscriber, when the doors were thrown open—but had since that period sold out.

Had the members who spoke against the present report, made good their charges against the bank, he had determined to vote with them, although not convinced of the propriety of the house assuming judicial powers. But the charges were not made good.

There were, he said, two modes by which the interests of agriculture could be promoted ; by a loan office, and by the bank, which latter, furnishing the merchants with money, procured a ready sale for produce. As a farmer, he had experienced the good consequences of it. The other, by ena-

bling

bling the farmer to borrow money for the improvement and cultivation of his lands, greatly advanced his interests.

Mr. Whitehill. One of the city members has remarked, that he believes, if an angel from heaven were to endeavour to convince me, it would have no effect: if an angel spoke as he has done, I should regard him as a fallen angel.

He has said, that farmers or millers may be accommodated with loans by the bank. But can any farmer in Lancaster or Cumberland derive benefit from loans for forty-five days? They cannot come here to renew their obligations.—Facts are stubborn things.

He also says that notwithstanding the cry of the country people for paper money, they will not receive it in payment for their produce. I have received it equal to gold or silver for produce. Perhaps others are afraid: and indeed when we hear a gentleman of such wealth and influence declare that he puts it away as fast as he can, for fear of depreciation, is it not enough to shake the credit of the paper money?

The gentleman has said that industry is promoted and manufactures encouraged by the bank: but loans at forty-five days will do neither the one nor the other.

It has been observed, that the bank has not a capital of ten millions of dollars, and that therefore no danger is to be apprehended on that head. But it might have had that capital by the charter: why then should we restore it?

A gentleman has in answer to me remarked, that it was impossible for the legislature which granted the charter, to know the bye-laws of the bank. I ask, then, was it not absurd to give a charter empowering the corporation to make such bye-laws as they pleased?

The bank, for aught we know, might have become a trading company; and, by stopping discounts, at particular times, might take advantage of the private merchants——

Mr. Fitzsimons. The corporation is restrained from trading by the charter.——

Mr. Whitehill demanded—by what charter?

To this mr. Fitzsimons replied by the charter of congress.

Mr. Whitehill. This is nugatory. The charter of congress is of no avail here. Congress had no power to grant any charter—and in this instance stepped out of their line. If that was all the restraint on the president and directors, they might have become a trading company when they pleased.

I

The

The bank, it is hinted, enables the merchant to purchase produce—and the farmer consequently gets a better price. But flour was three dollars per hundred, before the revolution, and it is not much higher now. The whole business is reduced to this: when the danger of the bank monopolizing trade is urged, the charter of congress is pleaded; and we are told that the state is safe. But this is a nullity. Let the bank go on, as it stands at present. The people who deal in it will be safer. If the money in the vaults is not sufficient, the estates of the subscribers will be responsible. This has been observed already—and not a word has been offered in answer to it. Is it not better have two or three equal banks, and then the citizens will be courted for their custom, than one which can do as it may see fit?

Mr. Woods said if the gentleman's observation, that the charter was but a mere piece of paper, which the house might burn at pleasure, was true, the constitution was also a piece of paper, and might with equal justice be burned; if that was the case, God help poor Pennsylvania! Those gentlemen who pretended to be constitutionalists, thought themselves exempt from attending to the constitution—They made it a nose of wax, which they twisted at pleasure.

Mr. R. Morris. I did not intend to have risen again on this question: but as some new matter has occurred, I think it may not be improper to offer a few additional observations.

A member has remarked upon the manner in which the question was proposed by the chairman of the committee whose report is under debate—viz. " whether they were wil-
" ling to give such information as was not inconsistent with
" the secrecy of that institution?" He has from this drawn an inference that any application from the committee of the late house would have been fruitless, on account of this secrecy. But herein he is much deceived: this secrecy relates to the state of accounts depending between individuals and the bank: and the necessity of this secrecy every one must see. I appeal to the feelings of all who hear me, whether they would choose the state of their accounts should become known to any but those officers of the bank to whom they are confided? The depositors of money there, would no more have their deposits made public than if the cash remained in their chests: and much less would those who stand indebted, consent to have the state of their accounts known to any but those with whom the debt is contracted.

As

As superintendent of finance, I was entitled to receive daily a state of the accounts of the bank: but neither the directors nor myself ever considered this as extending to the accounts of individuals: and I never was made acquainted with any such matter. This is the only kind of secrecy, I apprehend, that could have been meant by the committee, or that could be necessary for the president and directors to observe; for as to the state of their own affairs, that is, the affairs of the bank generally, I take it, they would, whenever needful or proper, explain them without hesitation.

Upon the doctrine of charters, the gentleman insists that they cannot be taken away in the courts of law: in which I agree, that unless there be a forfeiture on the part of the corporation, they cannot.

I shall not, however, dwell upon this subject—but proceed to the proposal for mortgaging certain revenues to the bank. That proposal did not go to the extent gentlemen are pleased to mention. One member has remarked that it is very extraordinary such a proposal should have been made without the knowledge of the president and directors; and added, that if such was the case, it was an insult to the house.

That proposal was made by a member of this house, who had a right to make it: and if the house had agreed to that proposal, they must, as he mentioned at the time, have appointed a committee to negociate and settle the affair with the president and directors of the bank. Surely there was nothing like an insult in this.

I shall pass over the assertions that the impost and taxes would not have been sufficient to pay the public creditors, with observing that if they had been duly collected, there would have been in the treasury a sum fully adequate.

It has been insisted that usury has been coeval with the bank. Usury sprung up on the decease of the continental money; and if I had expected the charge to have been renewed and insisted on, I might have brought evidence of the fact. I am satisfied that some of the brokers' books would shew it, and probably those might be obtained without much difficulty.

The member from Fayette seems to charge me with claiming the merit of bringing about the revolution. In this, however, no part of my conduct will justify him. It is not my practice to claim merits which do not belong to me. It is true, in defending myself from attacks which have been made, I have been obliged sometimes to mention services performed; and by so doing, they are submitted to public investigation, and would be contradicted, if not truly stated. When I mentioned the supplies of flour sent to general Washington's camp, it was introduced to shew the distresses of the times: however, I did not, as this gentleman was pleased to express himself, say it was sent at my expence; but that it was obtained upon my credit: neither has my vanity or folly ever prompted me to pretend that I established the independence of America. It is my glory to have had a share in it; and I am not ashamed of the share which has fallen to my lot; I hope it will ever do me honour.

As to the claims made by the author whom the gentleman mentioned, I know nothing about them. I shall not contest his claims, nor those of any other person. Whoever have deserved well of their country, or think they have done so, shall not be disturbed by me. There are thousands and thousands who have been honourably concerned: and I am as ready to give to each his share of merit, as I am to receive even what credit that gentleman himself will allow me.

In this house we enjoy the freedom of speech: every member may deliver what sentiments he pleases; and, if he chooses, he may attack characters without being accountable to any tribunal, provided he observes the decency and decorum due to the house: but I cannot refrain from a wish that it were laid down as a rule, never to abuse this privilege, by attacking those who cannot speak here, and of course have it not in their power to defend themselves. I am led to these observations, by the gentleman having introduced into his speech an author, who, he says, is unprincipled, hires out his pen for pay, and who, in walking the market place, without money in his pocket, finds a five shilling bill, steps into a tavern, procures with it a dinner, &c. and then exclaims, this paper money, after all, if it be not money, is to me victuals and drink. This author, whoever he is, is not on this floor; and consequently cannot do himself justice here. Whether he is paid or not, I cannot say. He is not in my pay: nor do I know any that do pay him: for, if I guess right at the person, I can pretend to nothing more than common acquaintance, and the intercourse of common civility which has arisen in consequence of his long residence here, and which originated in his public services. But I feel for his situation, in this instance, having been, in the same manner, attacked on this floor, when I could not be permitted to repel those attacks, as I had not then a seat

in

in assembly. I do not reproach the member for using the freedom of speech—but I wish more delicacy were observed. If the author in question has been guilty of any impropriety, there are proper places to bring him to punishment, and in which he can be admitted to make his defence.

It has been observed in this debate, that the directors of the bank being chosen by the stockholders,—and these voting according to property,—the directors are elected by six or seven men, largely concerned in stock: and this manner of voting is strongly objected to. I ask what should give the right of voting in such an institution, but property? Shall those who hold a small number of shares, have equal votes with those who hold a great number? You may as well pass an Agrarian law, and divide the property. Who would invest their money in such an institution, if that regulation were to take place? Voting according to property is the only proper mode of election, although a deviation has taken place. Shall a man with a fortieth part of the interest in bank stock which another holds, have an equal voice with him in the election of those who are to manage that interest? Surely not. It has been said that the directors exercise a tyranny over the stockholders. I wish it had been shewn how: their continuance in office is given as a reason: and it is urged that they may remain in office as long as they live, which would be a species of tyranny. Their continuance in office is a proof that they enjoy the confidence of the stockholders—not that they tyrannize over them. However, a change in the direction was intended: and a number of the stockholders went to the late election, with intent to vote-in some new hands. But the attack on the bank seeming to render its duration doubtful, they re-elected the same gentlemen, in order that if the business were to be closed, it might be done by those who, having so long conducted it, were best acquainted with it.

The eleventh and thirteenth articles of the proposals for establishing the bank, published with my name thereto, are brought forward by the member from Fayette, to shew that my sentiments are changed respecting the control of government over this institution. The clause subjecting the state of the bank accounts to the inspection of the superintendent of finance, was then excellent and highly approved, because I was the superintendent—but now, he remarks, I thank God it is not under the control of government. I am still of opinion that the clause was excellent, and that it was useful.

The institution was framed under an expectation that the public monies were to be placed there from time to time—and that it would derive advantage from the public funds passing through that channel. It was therefore judged proper for the bank to submit to such inspection, and necessary to create public confidence—first, because the public money being deposited there, the united states would, by their officer, know that it was secure: and secondly, individuals having transactions with the bank, would think themselves safe, and believe in its stability, whilst it enjoyed the confidence of government, and its proceedings were subject to such a check as the inspection of them by a public officer of high trust. These are the considerations that induced my approbation to those clauses then. But what is the case now? The united states have no longer a superintendent, and although they have a board of treasury with the same powers, they have no funds in the bank: therefore no necessity exists of any examination into the state of that institution on their part: and with respect to individuals, it has fully acquired the necessary confidence: so that in neither case is this inspection any longer necessary.

If, indeed, the state of Pennsylvania had thoughts of depositing money in the bank, the government might talk of control; and would have a right to make terms. They might stipulate as a condition, that the treasurer of the state, or some other of their officers, should so far have inspection of the bank, as to know, before the treasurer, the collectors of taxes, of imposts, of duties, of excise, &c. should deposit public monies there, that such deposits would be perfectly secure: and I am persuaded that the president and directors would have no objection to the appointment of such an officer, to whom, in such case, they would freely communicate a state of the general accounts of the bank. This kind of connection between government and the bank, would be very proper: but any subjection or dependence of the bank on the government, would be inconsistent with its nature.—The attempt, then, to prove any inconsistency in my opinions fails—my present being perfectly consistent with my former opinions on this point.

As to what I said respecting members receiving per centage for transacting business in the land-office, I do not know it of my own knowledge—but by information: and I have
a paper

a paper in my hand, stating that a member of this house will, if called upon, prove the fact.

The gentleman said that this information was addressed to the gallery. But if the gallery had been cleared, and the doors of this house closed, I should have gone into the same explanation that I have done in the course of this business. It is true, I rejoice that so many of my fellow citizens are present at these debates: as they will probably, from the explanations respecting the bank, become better acquainted with the nature of it, than many of them were before; and it only wants to be understood, to make it fully and clearly seen how much the interest of every man in the state may be or is benefitted by it.

It has in the course of this debate been more than once asserted, that the paper money of the state, is depreciated by the bank. This I deny totally. The paper money is received on deposit at the bank, at considerable expence and trouble: one or more clerks at handsome salaries, are necessary for the receiving and paying it, and for keeping accounts with the depositors. The president and directors of the bank do all this without an iota of profit—being prompted thereto by a desire of supporting the credit of that paper they are charged with depreciating. From the third of June 1785, to the twenty-eighth of February in the present year, they received of this paper on deposit 104,460l. 18s. 4d. From the twenty-eighth of February, to the present day, they have received 2819l. 15s. 8d.—making in the whole 107,280l. 14s. And the credit of this account is,—For sundries paid from the third of June 1785, to the twenty-eighth of February, 97,767l. 15s. 6d. ditto paid from the first to the twenty-eighth of March, 3520l. 11s. 6d.—Balance remaining on hand, 5992l. 7s. From this statement it appears, that the whole amount of the emission, that for the loan-office excepted, has already passed through the bank: for this, accounts have been opened in bank for sixty-seven persons.— I hope it will not be asserted that all these pains are taken in order to destroy the credit of the paper money. I have already answered the charges against myself on this subject, —although perhaps it might have been as well to pass them by, as I have done others, in silent contempt.

The gentleman from Fayette with much modesty, declares, he does not pretend to an equal degree of understanding with us. We, however, admit that he has it, and the contest between us, is an acknowledgment, on our part, of

his

his poffeffing equal abilities : but I hope this modefty was not affumed to extort compliments from us.

The gentleman fays, he hopes the members of this houfe are not capable of being corrupted. I hope with him that they are not. I have no fufpicions of the kind—nor ever had, But members of affembly are liable to be influenced in their conduct, as well as other men. However, whether they are or are not, I have never made an attempt to influence any one of them; nor can any one fay, that I have ever held a converfation, done, or faid a fingle thing to influence his vote upon any queftion whatever.

Mr. Smilie. The worthy member gave the houfe to underftand, that if it were not for fome people, we would not now be oppofed to the bank, On this I remarked, that if we were capable of being corrupted, thofe on our fide of the queftion had not the means of corruption in their hands.

Mr. R. Morris. As there are perfons out of doors prejudiced againft the inftitution, it is natural for them to exert all their influence to injure it. They get hold of the members—and tell them fine ftories, make ftrong affertions, and by degrees lead them into their fnares, by means of deception, without any attempt at corruption; and this is by no means uncommon. It is well known that mankind are flaves to prejudices—and to prejudices frequently not their own—but fuch as are taken up on the credit of others. I thank God our legiflature is incorruptible, I believe it has always been fo: and I hope it will ever fo continue—at leaft we have one fecurity for it—I cannot fee how or for what it would be worth while to corrupt them, were they fo difpofed. If in this or any other part of the debate, when animated with the fubject, I have not treated the members oppofed to me with all the decency and decorum they could wifh, I fhould be forry for it—as being contrary to my intention: but I am not fenfible that any fuch thing has efcaped me. Indecencies may tend to inflame—but they feldom convince.

The fame gentleman fays, he refpects my private character—but muft differ from me in politics. I wifh we could agree in our political opinions: it might be of fome advantage to the ftate; but as we cannot, we muft be content—he to hold his opinions—and I to enjoy mine.

Some expreffions which have dropped from this gentleman and from the member from Cumberland, feem to imply, that had the report before us, propofed any modification of the bank charter, it might have met with their approbation—
but

but that in its present form, it is inadmissible. I do not see how the committee could have made a report of that kind: they certainly were not authorised to do it. It has been fully proved that the repealing law does not rest on the same support as our other laws: it is not founded in truth and fact—but in the preamble the reverse is asserted: and this is of itself a sufficient cause for repealing that repealing law.

I am not willing to take up more of the time of this house: it would be going over again the same beaten track. We are pretty well tired of the subject by this time: and I hope the question will soon be put. I hope that no doubts remain as to the utility of the bank. I trust it has been clearly proved, that it has never been injurious to the safety or welfare of the state in any shape or way.

Mr. Finlay. Had my arguments of yesterday, been stated justly, and replied to with fairness, I would not have thought it necessary further to detain this house—as the attention of the members is, I conceive, already wearied out. I have, doubtless, been unhappy in speaking less distinctly or less audibly than usual, so as to occasion them to be unjustly stated. The manner in which I then investigated the case, has been made an honourable mention of by the gentlemen on the other side of the debate; but could I ascribe the treatment my arguments met with, in stating them yesterday, from a gentleman of eminent discernment [mr. Morris] to artifice, it would be a more flattering circumstance, than any eulogiums the gentleman has been pleased to bestow. However, candour obliges me to acknowledge that the gentleman who spoke first this morning [mr. Fitzsimons] replied to some of my arguments with ability, stated them fairly, and answered sensibly. And there are, certainly, many good arguments respecting the conveniency of the bank, that may apply in its favour: and it is the duty of this house to compare the arguments arising either from its utility or its mischief—its safety or its danger—and by giving each of them due weight, to observe how the balance turns.

I shall now proceed to mention some instances of the treatment my arguments met with yesterday; and then prosecute some observations which I touched but slightly at the first—and also some which I then waved.

My first argument was entirely mis-stated. Knowing that the preamble of the report under debate, contains reasoning totally improper and disgraceful, I thought it would have been

been an infult to the dignity of the houfe to argue upon it, which I therefore declined, alleging, that though the reafons affigned by the committee of the late houfe, for repealing the charter, were infufficient, yet, if fufficient reafons do now exift in the nature of the cafe, their decifion ought not to be repealed. This I illuftrated by judicial examples ; and alluded to legiflative ones, of which I fhall now mention one. In the act lately paffed for opening the road by the Water Gap, the reafon affigned, is, that there is no road there. Surely, this is not the true reafon, although it is the only one affigned by this houfe : for if that were the true and a fufficient reafon, it would imply that this houfe ought to make fpecial laws for opening roads in all places where they are wanted, which is, by ftanding laws, the bufinefs of the county courts. The true reafon muft have been not only the utility of that road, but the broken and uninhabited ftate of that country. But the gentleman alleged that I applied this argument to the refolution now before the houfe.

I mentioned agrarian laws merely on account of the ufe the gentleman had made of them, in alleging that the charter of the bank could not be taken away without admitting agrarian laws. I obferved that though wealth was not equal enough in this ftate to the genius of our government, yet to admit thofe laws was improper; and, under our government, would be unjuft : but that they had nothing to do with the prefent cafe, which was not taking away property—was not touching the cafh of the proprietors of the bank—but folely repealing a law which gave an undue and impartial advantage to one fet of men. How could the gentleman's fears be alarmed from this ? How could he fay that I alleged though agrarian laws were not juft now proper, that they would be fo fome fhort time hence ? It was the gentleman himfelf introduced the term : and I only attempted to refcue it from the improper ufe he had made of it.

I mentioned as an argument the unfuitablenefs of fuch an inftitution to the government, laws, and habits of this ftate. The gentleman ftated that I had faid it was contrary to law. Surely, if a difputant has the power to make his antagonift fay what he pleafes, he may eafily reply : fo the gentleman has done. He fays it was not contrary to law—becaufe the charter was a law. It was not contrary to habit—for the people had a habit of applying at the bank for difcounts, and

and carrying their money there to depofit it. I beg now to repeat and enforce fome of my arguments on that head.

The frame of government of this ftate, being the great deed of truft between thofe in government and the citizens at large, is a charter of the firft importance; and circumfcribes and contains all other charters that can lawfully exift: yet it is a charter for only feven years. It is not only fubject to change, as all other governments are, by natural right—but it muft, by the law of its own exiftence, be brought to the teft feptennially. And can the legiflature give charters more facred and more permanent than the government itfelf? No: the very nature of things forbids it. By our laws, all eftates, real or perfonal, are divifable; the grand fource and fupport of feudal dignity are therefore taken away—fince by law, every child, with one fmall exception, enjoys an equal fhare: and our habits with refpect to teftaments perhaps correfpond more perfectly with our laws, than thofe of any other country in the world. Our real eftates are fubject to be fold for debts; and are actually daily felling in this manner. In a country, where we have no wealthy incorporated companies of merchants—where we have no nobles with great eftates, permanent in the family line—where we have no royal prerogative fupported by an enormous civil lift and numberlefs dependents—I fay in a country where we have no counterpoife to correct its influence or control its enormities by their own—fhall we grant fuch an inftitution? Shall we give fuch an artificial fpring to congregated wealth? By no means. It was in this manner I argued its inconfiftence with the fpirit of our laws, &c. and not in the manner ftated by the gentleman.

My arguments on the ufefulnefs of the bank—and the examples by which I illuftrated them—were treated in the fame manner. But this houfe heard my arguments and the manner in which the gentleman accommodated them to his replies: therefore I fhall not refcue them; but fhall juft obferve, that I acknowledged freely the ufefulnefs of the bank—I gave it all the credit I thought it deferved: but did the gentleman acknowledge the ufefulnefs of paper money or a loan office? Did he give paper money one grateful compliment for the good it has at any time done? No—he did not.

I forbore yefterday faying much about paper money or a loan office—as things fufficiently underftood: but I beg leave now to offer a few further obfervations refpecting them. By the laft emiffion we have anticipated our revenue, and fo

made

made a faving to the ftate ; by it we have relieved our fuffering creditors ; by it we have brought in our revenues, and filled our treafury, which had for years groaned with emptinefs. By means of the fpring it gave to circulation, it brought in more fpecie than we could have otherwife got. By means of it, the gentleman anfwerable to his wifhes, will get more old debts paid in to him ; and, anfwerable to his diffidence, he acknowledges he can put it away again immediately. By the laft emiffion, Pennfylvania has recovered her dignity ; and fhewn herfelf to be poffeffed of that wifdom which pervaded her counfels whilft fhe was a colony.

The inftitution of a loan-office is one of the moft mafterly ftrokes of national good fenfe : the advantages of the prefent one, though fo new in its operations, have been of amazing fervice. Vaft numbers of our citizens were in debt to the ftate for their lands, which they held by occupancy only : thofe people have been enabled to pay their debts to the ftate ; and to affift the public creditors, by increafing the demand for their certificates. I will mention one inftance :—as I was coming to this city laft week, I met with a man who had patented his own land, and procured a loan of one hundred pounds. In confequence of orders I had with me, I received about half his loan ; and brought it back to pay for the lands of others. Thus it not only pays an intereft, but finks a treble intereft.

A loan-office, at this time, is not only a fource of revenue, to the amount of the net intereft it brings ; but has contributed by raifing the demand, to raife the public certificates from 3s. 9d. to 6s. : and as every pound value of them laid out as above, takes off an intereft from three to four for one, by finking fuch a proportion of the public debts—it is one of thofe honourable and ufeful kinds of fpeculation, fraught with advantage both to the ftate and to individuals ; and gives the fureft fund for the redemption of paper money. The inftitution of a bank, on the other hand, as I faid before, increafes ufury ; promotes the fpirit of monopoly ; and, in our prefent fituation, prevents improvements and equal circulation of money.

All the gentlemen on the other fide of the queftion, deny that it promotes ufury. Let us examine this a little. Does it not give a facility to trade ? Is not this its proper ufe ? Is not the balance of trade againft us ? Does it not, therefore, give facility to importation in a degree too great for our exportation ? Surely, it does. When gentlemen obtain the affiftance

—the

—the ready and generous affiftance of the bank, to purchafe imported goods—muft they not pay at a fhort and a certain day? And when the market is glutted with goods, and the appetite of the confumer cloyed, what fhall—what can the borrower do? He may and often does go to the vendue ftores, and lofe his property by ready money fales, at the rate of 50s. a minute: or he may go to the rapacious brokers, whofe exiftence in Philadelphia is coeval with the bank, and of them borrow at five or fix per cent. per month. This has been the relief, no lefs common than deftructive—the mournful relief of thofe who have with the beft defigns and flattering expectations, made ufe of the delufory affiftance of the bank: and thus it is likely to be with every inftitution inconfiftent with the laws and manners of a people.

But this is not all: the bank, it is certain, takes a kind of compound intereft itfelf: and when fimple intereft requires about feventeen years to enable one million of dollars to grow into two——the method practifed by the bank (fuppofing the holders not to draw their dividends) would make one million produce above fix in about 26 years: and to follow this thought for a century to come, how amazing the idea! In the bank money is arrefted. It muft increafe, without a poffibility of becoming lefs. It is fecured by fuch a charter from every rifk, and guarded againft every danger but what may arife from the poffible villainy of the conductors of its operations.

As wealth is the means of conducting—as wealth is the means of obtaining monopolies—even when in the hands of jarring individuals—how much more muft it facilitate fuch defigns, when in the hands of a permanent fociety, congregated by fpecial privilege, and actuated by the principles of united avarice? Let us fuppofe for a moment, that I poffeffed the greateft real eftate under the government, and that I had likewife the greateft commercial wealth, and confequently a greater credit in all commercial countries than any other citizen in the ftate, and that I had the greateft number of fhares in, and confequently the greateft influence over the bank, would not I in this cafe have it in my power to monopolize the moft valuable foreign markets, and to fay who fhall and who fhall not trade? Would it not be in my power to fix the rate of exchange as I pleafed—fo that when in the natural courfe of trade it fhould be 163 or 170, I could raife

it to

it to 175 or 180? I could increase the necessity of remitting by bills, and avail myself of that necessity.

The bank in the present state of things, prevents even the improvement of this city. Houses and lands have been sold, and their price locked up in the bank, where it is free from taxes, and where it increases without the labour of the owner. Thus by discouraging improvements, it prevents population, and with it the rising glory and strength of the commonwealth. An equal circulation of the signs of wealth, tends to promote equal interests—equal manners—and equal designs: but the situation and circumstances of few countries admit of equal circulation: yet surely government ought not to give its special aid to render circulation necessarily unequal. However this is an argument well understood, and has been spoken to formerly.

One gentleman [mr. Morris] would persuade us that the transfers of stock prevent the dangers or cure the evils of the institution. How can this be? Will a few individuals transferring their bank stock, change the principles—the nature—and influence of the institution? By no means; but this is too plain a case to dwell upon; and has already been well spoken to.

Against the right of the legislature to dissolve such charters, it has been often said that that body might as well disannul the patents of our lands: and for the same purpose, agrarian laws have been, I think, rather improperly mentioned. What do these arguments mean? Is dissolving the charter of the bank, and entering into it, to take away the gold and silver from the owners, for the public use, the same thing? Surely no. But the right of the legislature is so clearly confessed by gentlemen of legal knowledge—it is so essential to the safety of government—and has already been so well spoken to—that it would perhaps be an insult to the good sense of this house, to say any thing further on this head.

Much has been said by gentlemen on the other side of the question, respecting the advantage arising from the bank to the farmer, the mechanic, &c.—It seems to be denied that the balance of trade is against us; or that the bank promotes that unfavourable balance. One gentleman [mr. Fitzsimons] supposes that I stated the exports from Pennsylvania too low: I believe he did not hear me well—for in every other mention of my arguments, he did me justice. I will therefore repeat my sentiments on that head. We export flour— but not so much as formerly: this is owing, among other things,

things, to a scarcity of labouring people: the drain of young men during the war, and for many years having so few emigrants, accounts for this. We export flaxseed, though not so much of it as usual: the binding of our lands, through long working, and the change of seasons, together with people depending more upon hemp, accounts for this. That the lumber trade must continue to decay, requires no investigation to account for it. What else of consequence does Pennsylvania export? Nothing, I believe, worth enumerating: yet we have the foundations of commerce, which rising ages will doubtless improve. I perfectly agee with the gentleman that it is our duty to cultivate the mutual interest of the farmer, the mechanic, and the merchant; but how is this to be done? We have been told we ought to alter the balance of trade, &c. but in the present state of things, we may as well talk of turning the stream of the Delaware. To cultivate these now jarring interests, and render them mutual, we must first propagate or import a greater number of people, that we may have labour of all sorts cheaper; we must encourage our own produce and manufactures; we must try to curb our luxury—to mortify our madness for trade and foreign wares. Our present manner of trading, if persisted in, must prevent us from ever being in any reputable degree, an independent or a commercial nation; still it is said that the balance of trade is not so much against us; but I ask any gentleman acquainted with it, if the rate of exchange is not against us? I ask is not the rate of exchange the touchstone of trade—and the infallible criterion which side the balance turns to? It shews the price of money. Is not the rate of exchange more against us than before the bank existed? I believe it is; and the influence of the bank is well calculated to keep it so. I wish for a commerce built upon the foundation of population and industry; every other kind of commerce must be ruinous, and ought to be discouraged.

The trade of Amsterdam has been mentioned by a gentleman, and applied to our case; but I canot see any similarity. It is true, the people of Amsterdam have very little of the produce of their own country to trade upon; but they make the materials of almost all the world their own—so as to promote population and industry; they are in a great degree the mechanics, the factors, and the carriers of Europe; and their wealth is the envy even of London herself. But we neither manufacture nor carry for ourselves—nor do we get rich.

A gentleman

A gentleman from the city [mr. Fitzſimons] has mentioned the cheap bargains overtrading and uſury have given
many an opportunity of obtaining : but I ſhould have
thought this a ſufficient argument on the other ſide. Is it not
an evidence of the evils about which we complain ? Is it not
the cauſe of the ruin of many ?
  The great amount of the impoſt received laſt year is alſo
uſed as an argument : certainly this is an inconteſtible evidence to my purpoſe. We received 100,000l. of an impoſt :
and we may preſume that much eſcaped the notice of the
officers : and the impoſt a part of that time was low : how a-
mazingly, therefore, muſt our imports have exceeded our
exports ! I ſuppoſe the difference could not have been leſs
than fifty, perhaps a hundred to one. Can any nation long
exiſt, conducting ſuch a trade ? The gentleman mentions
the vaſt improvements occaſioned in Scotland by banks ſince
their eſtabliſhment. I believe Scotland has received benefit
from banks : but our circumſtances and thoſe of Scotland
are very different ; and though I am not ſufficiently informed to be able to deſcribe the banks of Scotland, I know they
are neither chartered nor conducted like the late bank, now
under debate.
  A worthy member [mr. Morris] in his arguments in favour of the bank told this houſe, that I alſo loved wealth,
and purſued it—Doubtleſs I do. I love and purſue it—
not as an end, but as a means of enjoying happineſs and
independence ; and ſo far I am for enjoying it. Though
I have it not in any proportion to the degree of what
the worthy gentleman has informed us of himſelf—yet I
have more land than I can make a proper uſe of, and not
a great deal leſs than I wiſh to have, though I purchaſed it
at ſecond hand. I have enough of wealth to give a ſpring
to induſtry ; and to procure the neceſſaries and a competence
of the comforts of life. But he has ſaid that I follow land-
jobbing ; that he has ſeen me in the land office ; and that
if I did not procure lands for myſelf, I charged com-
miſſion upon doing it for my neighbours. I denied theſe
charges with perhaps too much warmth—not becauſe they
were diſgraceful—but becauſe they were, as applied to me,
miſtaken ; the gentleman has told us to-day that he is able
to prove the charge againſt ſome one perſon. I wiſh the
perſon was produced, and the charge proved ; I ſhould in-
ſiſt on the proof being brought forward, but from a con-
ſciouſneſs that it will not apply to me—and from an opinion
that it was improperly introduced into the preſent debate.
                                                               However

However, I believe, if members of this house are meant, the instances are rare; and I should have passed the whole as a piece of humour, but for the opportunity it gives me of offering a short but true picture of the situation of many of my constituents. Living as they do, in a new settlement, after having encountered the accumulated woods of ages, and beasts ravenous by nature, and rendered still more so by the unbounded extent of their range, they had scarcely made openings round their abodes—they had not banished the beasts of prey—when men more fierce, more cruel than the beasts, desolated their new raised dwellings, and spread destruction far and wide. Now, when they are returned, and feebly repairing the ruins of their dreary wastes, they find themselves in debt to the state for the very lands in defending which many of them lost their dearest friends and all their wealth. They endeavour—they strive with arduous diligence to pay the state its due: and, to be able to call the lands their own, they sell the last cow and sheep, to procure a little money (for nothing but cows and sheep will find money there). I myself have been urged to take the last cow—to take any thing they had, in order to secure their lands. They raise the last shilling they are able—and plead, as if for life, that we may add a few dollars to the scanty sum; and these are the people from whom the gentleman seems to think I take enriching commissions; but all the generous feelings of the human soul forbid such means of obtaining wealth; and it is a method much better suited to the habits of a merchant than a farmer.

One argument much used on the other side of the debate, I beg leave, altho' it has been well replied to already, to notice a little further. It respects the number of petitioners who have now brought this matter (it is said) before the house—it is emphatically called the voice of the people. In addition to what other gentlemen have justly observed upon this argument, I would further remark, that in every government (even the most absolute) the popular opinion, if not immoral, is the voice of God; but in Pennsylvania, it is not only formally but in fact the voice of the government—the government being solely founded on the popular authority; and the legislature being authorised and instructed to speak the popular voice, they are necessarily supposed to speak the voice of the people; one exception may be admitted, viz. if some new case arise, or if some new information is obtained, the majority of the people instructing and informing their reprefentatives, ought to be attended to. But is this the cafe in the prefent debate? By no means. The petitioners do not amount to one twentieth of our conftituents; and under all the influence that the nature of the inftitution cannot fail to produce on the human mind, furely it is wonderful, every thing confidered, that a much greater number of petitioners was not obtained, and ftrange that the gentlemen fhould make ufe of the few that are obtained, as an argument; but the cafe is too plain to be dwelt upon.

Having laboured arguments too long, which are clear in themfelves, and, I truft, well underftood in this houfe—I fhall juft obferve that as fome of them have been mis-ftated, a few inftances of which I have mentioned—and fome others replied to with candour and ability—and as the two gentlemen who have rifen in anfwer, have made honourable mention of my general arguments, but ftated their objections—I have ground to believe that thofe obfervations of mine which have not been replied to, are admitted; and, indeed, as they were drawn from the nature of things, I think they were unanfwerable—for things will ever operate according to their nature.

We are one great family: and the laws are our common inheritance. They are general rules, and common in their nature. No man has a greater claim of fpecial privilege for his £.100,000 than I have for my £5. No. The laws are a common property. The legiflature are entrufted with the diftribution of them. This houfe will not—this houfe has no right, no conftitutional power to give monopolies of legal privilege—to beftow unequal portions of our common inheritance on favourites.

This bank, the charter of which has been diffolved, and is now endeavoured to be renewed again, was truly an extraordinary creature. None like it does, I believe—none like it ever did exift in any nation: and furely fuch a being will never be reftored—will never be created again by the legiflature of this ftate. If we fhould reftore it, we would have no fecurity but in the moderation of the directors and ftockholders: but who will anfwer—who can be refponfible for future men—future times—and future events?

Mr. Clymer. Being confiderably indifpofed, I fhould not have taken any part in this day's debate, but that the report before us has been cavilled at. The gentleman from Fayette has again cenfured the charge in it, againft the committee of the late houfe for not making enquiry at the bank. Where
would

would have been the use of this, says he, does any one think the president and directors would have given any information against themselves? I will tell that gentleman its uses: It would have, at least, satisfied the forms of justice: and, had answers to proper questions been refused, it would have furnished more real matter against them, than any which has been alleged. The gentleman from Westmoreland has found it exceptionable in attacking the law on a wrong principle. When a law is once passed, says he, you should attend to its policy—and not to the means by which it was obtained—or, in effect, if the end be good, it shall sanctify the means. It has been a reproach to the order of the jesuits, that they held this doctrine: but I find there may be jesuits out of the Roman church. It is not taught by any presbyterian synod that I know of. It is not drawn from religion or morals—it is not the usual doctrine of the world, —near three thousand of our fellow citizens know nothing of it: they have, in their memorials to this house, omitted the policy of the law, to arraign the means of obtaining it— it was sufficient for them that the means were bad. The committee to whom their memorials were referred, have followed their example: they have proved that the late house were deceived by their committee—that the repealing law stands upon the falsest ground, the assumption in the preamble being absolutely without support from fact, and is not now contended for in argument: they are therefore fully justified in the conclusions they have drawn from those premises.

It was the least of my design to touch upon any thing but what concerned the report: but as the vote is, I suppose, to be immediately put, I would rectify the same gentleman's notion concerning the banks of Scotland, which he seems to think are banks of mortgage: as far as I have read or heard, there were two banks of discount at Edinburgh, which also lent on mortgage for a time, as long as they were able. Being obliged to drop the practice, the landholders, to supply their necessities, instituted a new bank at Ayr, for the sole purpose of lending on mortgage. But the long credit on such loans, soon reduced it to the greatest difficulties. It at length broke, and involved the whole country in ruin.

Previous to putting the question on the report, mr. Hannum moved to add to the resolution it contained, a direction to the committee to introduce a clause into the bill it recommended to be brought in, a clause subjecting the charter of the bank to proper regulations, restrictions and limitations.

This

This motion was negatived.—Yeas, 30—Nays, 39.

On the question, " will the house adopt the resolution submitted by the committee?" the yeas and nays were as follow, viz.

YEAS 28.

Robert Morris,
Thomas Fitzsimons,
George Clymer,
John Salter,
George Logan,
Wm. Robinson, jun.
Robert Ralston,
James Moore,
Thomas Bull,
John Hannum,
Samuel Evans,
Townsend Whelen,
Adam Hubley,
Alexander Lowrey,
Emanuel Carpenter,
Joseph Work,
Abraham Scott,
William Parr,
Henry Miller,
David M'Connaughty,
Michael Schmyser,
Philip Gartner,
Joseph Lilly,
Henry Tyson,
David M'Clellan,
Adam Eichelberger,
George Woods,
Samuel Wheeler,

NAYS, 41.

William Will,
James Irvine,
Isaac Gray,
John Clark,
Arthur Erwin,
John Smith,
Joseph Thomas,
Robert Smith,
Jonathan Morris,
Robert Whitehill,
John Carothers,
Frederick Watts,
John Creigh,
Abraham Lincoln,
Nicholas Lutz,
Henry Spyker,
Philip Kreemer,
Davis Davis,
Baltzer Gehr,
Robert Trail,
Peter Trexler, jun.
Peter Burkhalter,
Robert Brown,
John Piper,
Frederick Antis,
Samuel Dale,
William Todd,
William Finlay,
John Hughes,
John M'Dowell,
James Edgar,
John Smilie,
James M'Calmont,
Abraham Smith,
John Rhea,
Benjamin Rittenhouse,
Robert Lollar,
Adam Orth,
Robert Clark,
David Krouse,
Daniel Bradley,

So it was decided in the negative, and the report rejected.

FINIS.

www.ingramcontent.com/pod-product-compliance
Lightning Source LLC
Chambersburg PA
CBHW020100170426
43199CB00009B/350